THE APOSTLE JOHN
a blessed life

THE APOSTLE JOHN: a blessed life

Copyright © 2008 by James Byers

ISBN-10   0-9800285-2-3

ISBN-13   978-0-9800285-2-2

Edited by Jessa Rose Sexton

Cover design by Paula Rozelle Bagnall, inspired by Amy Davidson

Book Block design by Paula Rozelle Bagnall

Illustrations by Jennifer Savage

Published by:

O'More Publishing

A Division of O'More College of Design

423 South Margin St.

Franklin, TN 37064 U.S.A

Baptism is the <u>outward</u> <u>act</u> of Faith.
The spirit unites this outward act.

THE APOSTLE JOHN
a blessed life

James Byers

O'MORE
PUBLISHING

Thanks to all of my family and friends who offered words of encouragement, and especially to my wife, Marie, who offered many helpful suggestions along the way.

CONTENTS

PREFACE

My idea for writing this book developed as I was teaching an Asian class on Sunday mornings at the Harpeth Hills Church of Christ in Nashville, Tennessee. I found that John's writings, particularly the gospel and letters, became very suitable for study in such a class. My search for biographical material regarding John often proved to be somewhat disappointing. Even more difficult was the task of providing historical material relating to this apostle from the first century. Thus was conceived the writing of a concise biography of this unusual apostle that included a necessary synopsis of his writings without becoming another commentary. This book covers the time from John's early ministry to his writings in his later years. This is not a devotional study, but the reader may draw certain conclusions as to the effect that Jesus Christ had on this apostle. Others may find the historical data helpful in explaining at least a part of the Christian community of the Eastern Roman Empire during the first century. I used for scriptural references the Authorized Version in several cases, but I did not limit the text to one translation.

-James Byers

INTRODUCTION

H.E. Dana stated that the New Testament cannot be adequately interpreted without reference to the environment in which it was written.[1] By learning about the setting in which the Apostle John lived and wrote, as well as learning about the Apostle himself, we can more fully understand the Gospel inspired by God and written by this man, a man who truly led a blessed life.

THE SON OF ZEBEDEE

John the Apostle was truly the Christian of the first century. His life spanned the rule of Augustus Caesar through Trajan; thus he lived through the reign of twelve emperors and died during the rule of the thirteenth in the period of time known in Latin as the *Pax Romana* or Roman peace. He may have been the first Christian centenarian for he lived most if not all of the first century. If Jesus were born between 6 and 4 BC, John, assumed to be slightly younger, would have been born some three to five years later. From all traditional accounts, he died during Trajan's rule, somewhere after AD 98.

John was not only a survivor but managed to fill his life in what was later to be called a Renaissance style: he lived the life of a laborer, merchant, disciple, apostle, preacher, teacher, beloved elder, and writer. Of all the New Testament writers, he alone was proficient in the literary genres of biography, letters, and prophetic writing.

The age of Augustus

The Apostle Paul wrote in Galatians that Jesus came in the "fullness of time" or, to be more precise, the exact time in human history. The Greek word that Paul used was *pleroma* and can be translated as a completion, thus inferring a time that was correct according to God. Certainly, part of the completeness was political in nature. The rule of Augustus Caesar, which began in 27 BC and lasted through AD 14, became a defining time in ancient history. Rome began to dominate the classical world and unite it. Dana considered Augustus Caesar the greatest of the Roman emperors and one of the greatest of all statesmen. Indeed, as legend said, he found Rome a city of brick and left it a city of marble. With such a peace and the attending prosperity, Christianity became a world religion.

As before mentioned, John, as well as Jesus, lived during this time. To some degree John experienced the protection of Rome all of his life; Roman rule would permeate even the hills of Galilee. The emperor was known as the *Princeps* or first citizen of the empire and as the *pater patriae* or father of his people. With such imposing titles, Augustus turned the Mediterranean Sea into a Roman lake. He established and helped preserve a tradition that endured for centuries.

Other historians agree that the Augustan age was an ideal time for progress. Michael Grant considered Augustus one of the most talented, energetic, and skillful administrators that the world has ever known.[1] Ancient writers were most positive in their assessment. Tacitus gave Augustus high marks in law and order, centralization of government, lack of coercion, and the creation of government which fell short of a dictatorship. Even the sarcastic Seutonius conceded that Augustus, after a full life, was blessed with a peaceful death.[2] His rule totaled forty-one years of his seventy-seven year life. As Pat Southern surmised, "He had the capacity to make people believe in him, and then make them grateful."[3]

We can conclude that John, in his earlier years, lived during the same advantageous time as Jesus. While Jews were, for the most part, not citizens of Rome and exempt from military service, they were given the protection of the emperor during the reign of Augustus. He protected the Jewish people and adopted a general policy that a nation's customs, even religion, could be tolerated to keep an orderly empire.

Thus John's life began in a comparative period of tranquility as far as the empire was concerned.

John in Galilee

We must now turn to what we know of his early life and to the region called Galilee. From all evidence in the gospels, the Apostle John was a native of Galilee. The standard point for the beginning of Jesus' life was the census of the Governor Quirinius recorded by the writer Luke in the second chapter of his gospel. W. P. Armstrong in his article "Chronology of the New Testament" mentioned the possibility of several kinds of censuses. In particular Quirinius might have finished a census begun by his predecessors, or he might have been commissioned by Augustus. Armstrong also mentioned the theory that Quirinius "may have been an imperial procurator specially charged with authority in the matter of the Herodian census."[4] This census would have marked the birth of Jesus before the death of Herod which occurred in 4 BC.

It always has been interesting to question how well Jesus knew His disciples before the opening of His ministry. The gospel narratives have given no indication that Jesus had contact with the twelve although Jesus may have observed them in the fishing villages along the Sea of Galilee. Galilee itself was an ideal place for a Jewish youth to mature. Many articles past and present have described Galilee as the most beautiful and fertile region of Israel; the combination of mountains, hills, rolling plains, waterfalls, clear streams, lakes, and the vista of the snowcapped Mount Hermon confirmed these descriptions. The visitor today may see much the same landscapes and sites as Jesus and John.

This area was rich with fruitful soil producing the famed grapes of Carmel, countless olive trees, and the wheat fields of Chorazin. But Galilee was best known for its sea. The sea called Chinnereth in the Old Testament was described in the New Testament as Gennessaret or

..erias. The beauty of this small sea, that is only thirteen miles in length and seven in width, became famous as the locale for the teaching of Jesus. During His time, the sea was known by local fishermen as the source of their income. As Jesus grew up in Nazareth as the son of a carpenter, John grew up on the shores of the sea as the son of a fisherman. As a youth, John heard the stories of the heroes of this wonderful region. The judges Barak and Deborah and the prophets Elijah and Elisha were all part of the education of a Galileean. The ancient city of Megiddo and the mountain tops of Carmel and Gilboa were familiar to him.

The youth of John the Apostle was spent in this beautiful area under the firm rule of Augustus and Tiberius. Specifically John lived under the rule of Herod Antipas, one of the three sons of Herod the Great who had become tetrarch ruler of Galilee and Perea. According to Dana, Antipas was "diplomatic and conservative and was able to preserve relative peace."[5] His marriage to Herodias incurred the wrath of John the Baptist and resulted in a dark blot on his record. The Apostle John was probably unaware of Antipas' foibles until the appearance of John the Baptist. John the Apostle was more likely to be concerned with learning the craft of the fisherman, attending synagogue school, and participating in the three primary Mosaic feasts of Passover, Pentecost, and Tabernacles. All male children of the Jewish faith were required to attend these feasts after reaching their thirteenth birthday.

John's youth was spent as the child of Zebedee, a prosperous man who owned a successful fishing business on the shores of the Sea of Galilee. As Paul Butler commented, "Not one word in the gospels would give divine sanction to the ownership of property by a political state and Jesus Christ specifically and unequivocally approved of the ownership of property by individual persons." Butler's book about the Bible and civil government clearly showed that John and Jesus grew up in a mercantile society, tempered by the laws of charity according to the Mosaic principles.[6]

Although John showed a contemplative side in the gospel narratives and in his writings, there has been no evidence that he ever belonged to the ascetic groups that were in Israel at that time. The Essenes lived in the Dead Sea area; John was probably familiar with them and the Zelotai or Zealots, a political group. F. F. Bruce, the prominent church historian, dated the Zealots' rebellion against Rome as AD 6 when Judas the Galilean led a tax revolt against Quirinius, Legate of Syria. Bruce noted that John was obviously too young to participate, and there was no evidence of the civil rebel in him. Whether the Apostle Simon the Zealot was more inclined toward political rebellion or simply "a religious jealousy for the exclusive honor of Israel's God" as Bruce conjectured, we cannot say.[7]

Of course, another community centered near Qumran in the area of the Dead Sea was dedicated to ritual religious catharsis and was considered zealous for God. John did not seem to have been attracted to any of these groups and spent his youth by and on the sea. In a very real sense he became a man of nature in these surroundings. At night in his boat, he would have gazed on the beauty of the star-filled sky; by day, he was surrounded by the beauties of the spring-fed sea. He admired the enormous varieties of plant life and the lush grass and verdant landscape. Even as a man used to manual labor, he would have his moments of reflection.

Thus John and his brother James had conventional Jewish upbringings, reared by religious parents and guided by a strong work ethic. Coincidentally, Jesus had the same advantages.

We can also conclude that Galilee was sheltered from the turmoil of Judea during this time. Bruce wrote that the "troubles which beset Judea when it became a Roman province in AD 6 do not appear to have affected Galilee or Perea."[8] He did concede that all of the region was heavily taxed by Rome and agreed with the idea that taxation in the time of Jesus and John approached forty percent. All of this was dependent on the local

ruler, and Bruce and Dana acknowledge that Galilee had the ablest of
Herod's sons.

In such an environment the disciples of Galilee flourished. They were
exposed to a blending of Jewish and Hellenistic *(Greek)* cultures. During this
time, Antipas built the city of Tiberias in honor of the emperor, and John
lived to see the Sea of Galilee called the Sea of Tiberias. In those early
years he saw Tiberias grow to be a cultural center for both Gentile and
Jew. John was assuredly familiar with the town of Sepphoris which was
given the name Sebastus in honor of Augustus.

Luke recorded that Jesus began His ministry at the age of about thirty
years. As has been mentioned, the birth of Jesus can be placed before the
death of Herod in 4 BC. Assuming that Jesus was older than John, as is
the common perception, the apostle would have been about twenty-five
to thirty years of age at the beginning of this ministry.

The coming of Tiberius

The empire had changed from the early years. Augustus had died in AD
14 and Tiberius, his successor, was much more of a recluse. By the year
AD 26 he had retreated to the island of Capreae near modern Naples.
An increasing paranoia invaded the emperor's mind, and he became
extremely suspicious of all subordinates. He even became wary of his
most trusted advisor, Sejanus. Intrigue and debauchery became the
trademarks of the latter years of Tiberius. Tacitus, the foremost historian
of the time, thought Tiberius was evil to the core and wrote that after
the death of Sejanus, which was commanded by Tiberius, the emperor
retreated more into a dark world where "fear vanished and with it shame.
Thereafter he expressed only his own personality by unrestrained crime
and infamy."[9]

Michael Grant, a contemporary historian, concluded that Tiberius
did grow worse with age: "Although his mind remained clear enough for

most ordinary administrative purposes, his reason was almost unhinged by terror, self pity and the desire to avenge himself on those he believed were trying to break him."[10] Barbara Levick noted in her biography of this emperor, "Becoming more and more himself as he got older, he may even have come to relish the degradation and fear of the senators: impatience fell into cruelty. The man became harder and harder to reach, withdrawn on the island and into himself."[11] With the Roman Empire in turmoil, local rulers became more aggressive, even ruthless. Taxes, long a sore spot, became even more excessive. The Zealots became more of a force. Nationalism in Judea was on the rise, and Valerius Gratus was replaced by Pontius Pilate in the year AD 26.

John the Baptist

Before John met Jesus, he must have heard of another John, called the Baptist. The Baptist had openly challenged Roman rule by attacking the morals of Herod Antipas. Bruce observed that during the preaching of the Baptist, Antipas became very concerned with the message preached especially in regards to his marriage to Herodias.[12] John the Baptist reinforced the messianic hopes of the Jewish people, and although no documentation in the gospels located him in Galilee, he was preaching in the Perean part of the tetrarchy. Perhaps John the Apostle heard of the Baptist through travelers, or perhaps he had witnessed for himself the man from the wilderness. In his gospel he recorded John's baptizing people in the Jordan valley (John 1:28).

Of much concern to Herod Antipas was the large number of followers that the Baptist had. To a Roman puppet ruler, any large gathering could mean trouble. With Tiberius in self-proclaimed exile, each procurator or governor was on his own. Antipas could not afford the alienation of his subjects, and Bruce deduced that Antipas wanted the Baptist silenced. But the followers of the wilderness man were not silenced, and his words and actions were remembered. In the mind of Antipas must have lurked the fear of the messianic hope that continued to rise in the days of Jesus' ministry. The most popular view of the day concerning the Messiah was that of a warrior ruler who would unify the Jewish people and destroy their enemies, letting God's elect become conquerors. Dana concluded that no local ruler wanted such an uprising. Antipas in imprisoning and later executing the Baptist believed he could solve the problems of personal insult and potential revolution.[13]

We may conjecture that John the Apostle was also aware of such possibilities: he knew of the messianic hope, he had heard of the Baptist's teachings, and in his gospel he wrote of this man that introduced the ministry of Jesus. As a young fisherman, he heard the stories of the wild man of the desert regions. He very likely witnessed the Baptist proclaiming Jesus as the one who would take away the sins of humanity.

Conclusions could be drawn that John the Apostle did not live in complete isolation on his boat in the Sea of Galilee; he most assuredly would have received the education of the synagogue schools and certainly would have shared in the hope for a Messiah. John the Apostle saw and heard, from all indications, a man called the Baptist, the prophet from the desert wilderness, who drew large crowds wherever he preached. This was the life of the apostle at the time that Jesus began his ministry.

JAMES AND JOHN

Such inauspicious beginnings concealed the future of the Apostle John. No hidden talents were immediately revealed. He was described as a young fisherman working with his father, Zebedee, and his brother, James, plying the ancient trade of the sea. He was not rich, but neither was he poor. His earlier years, as is often the case in biblical accounts, were not recorded, his childhood was never mentioned, and we have only brief references about his father and mother. His father remained an obscure tradesman who must have earned a good living as a fisherman. His mother had a slightly different story.

It is Matthew who recorded an interesting intervention by John's mother in the twentieth chapter of his gospel. She boldly asked Jesus to promote her sons above the other disciples. These remaining disciples saw this as an obvious power play, but Jesus defused the situation with a wonderful lesson on the nature of greatness. Mark also mentioned this power struggle but chose to leave the mother out, though he did mention their mother at the cross, revealing her name: Salome (Mark 15:40).

Matthew mentioned John in the tenth chapter of his gospel. This time, as always, James received the prominence as the son of Zebedee with John listed as the brother of James. At this time Matthew recognized the Baptist as the John who was well-known. The Baptist was the great preacher, and Matthew would soon elevate him to the list of prophets which would include Elijah and Jeremiah (Matthew 16:14).

Jesus with James and John

Further in the book Matthew showed the special relationship that Jesus had with the brothers, the sons of Zebedee. In Matthew 17: 11–13, Jesus took the brothers with Simon Peter up to a high mountain where they witnessed His transfiguration. All of them saw Moses and Elijah revealed, and Peter offered to build tabernacles. Even at this time of euphoria, John was placed in obscurity and only mentioned as the brother of James. Matthew recorded another occasion when the brothers were in the private company of Jesus. At Gethsemane, Jesus took Peter and the "two sons of Zebedee" into the deeper recesses of this garden where He was to spend solemn hours in prayer. Unfortunately, these three fell asleep and were no consolation to Him (Matthew 26:36–46).

The gospels of Mark and Luke documented other references to the brothers that Matthew omitted. Mark recorded that Jesus gave the brothers the name Boanerges or "Sons of Thunder." Jesus quickly understood that the brothers were short-tempered. Many commentators have been content to award this dubious characteristic to Peter and only Peter. Mark also mentioned the brothers, along with Jesus and Peter, going to the house of the ruler of the synagogue where the ruler's daughter was raised from death (Mark 5:35–43). In Mark 13, Andrew joined the trio in asking Jesus when the temple would be destroyed.

Luke stated that James and John were Peter's partners in the fishing business. The Greek word is *koinonoi* and can be translated as people who share a common bond. Plummer translated the word partners in his commentary;[1] this word indicated the strong fellowship that continued among the three all of their lives. Luke also wrote of an incident when John told Jesus that he saw someone casting out demons in Jesus' name. John then congratulated himself by telling Jesus that he and others stopped the exorcism. This impulsive and self-centered action was quickly criticized by Jesus. Later in the same chapter, Luke recorded an even more unflattering picture of the brothers when he recalled that James and John wanted to incinerate an entire Samaritan village because they would not accept Jesus; Jesus told them He was not on earth to destroy (Luke 9:49–56).

Much later, Luke detailed the preparation that was assigned to Peter and John for the last Passover meal (Luke 27:7–13). This task included the arrangements for the upper room where all of the disciples shared their most intimate thoughts with Jesus. John was sent without James indicating that Jesus sensed a growing maturity in the future apostle.

The treatment of John by the other gospel writers is an interesting mixture. John was shown to be rash at times and then responsible in the

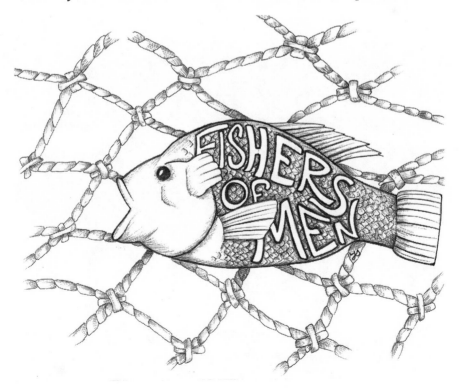

latter part of Jesus' ministry. He also began to assume his own identity; he was not just the son of Zebedee or the brother of James. Although not the natural leader that Peter was, neither was John a shriveled desert flower. Jesus saw in him an energy that burst forward, sometimes with inappropriate zeal. John's character continued to be refined.

JOHN ACCORDING TO JOHN

John wrote his gospel late in life. He was probably approaching seventy, looking back with long-term memory. Above all else, he remembered Jesus as the Word, or Logos, living with John and the other disciples as a real person (John 1:1–14). Strangely, he did not include himself or his brother James in his list of the disciples of Jesus (John 1: 37–51). In fact James was not mentioned in John's account of Jesus; however, Peter was in the story on almost every page of the closing chapters. Thus, it seemed that Peter was beginning to exercise more influence on John than his own brother.

Special favor with Jesus

At the most defining moment when the question of betrayal was being discussed, John revealed himself as finding special favor with Jesus, as being the one whom Jesus loved. In chapter 13, only John asked the question concerning the betrayer, and Jesus revealed this secret only to John. As we more closely examine the supper before the betrayal of Jesus, we can see where John was reclining on that fateful night. The table setting would be unusual to us, and contrary to Da Vinci's painting, the guests were reclining on couches. B. F. Westcott, the revered commentator, referred to Talmudic notes that showed that "the guests lay resting on their left arms, stretched obliquely." He added, "If three reclined together, the centre was the place of honour, the second place that above (to the left), the third that below (to the right). If the chief person wished to talk with the second, it was necessary for him to raise himself and turn around, for his head was turned away as he reclined." Westcott stated that Peter, who was in the second position, was not in a favorable place for hearing the whispers of Jesus.[1] Godet, in his commentary, remarked that John designated himself as a special disciple not through vanity but with infinite condescension.[2]

Later on when the arrest of their Lord was certain, John revealed that he was that other disciple who, with Peter, followed Jesus throughout the mock trial. John also indicated that he alone knew the high priest and went with Jesus into the courtyard with the permission of the religious rulers (John 18). There was much speculation that the family of Zebedee knew several of these leaders. The *Expositor's Greek Testament* expressed the opinion that John accompanied Jesus into the palace of Caiaphas, and that John, being known to Caiaphas, spoke to the doorkeeper to let Peter into the official residence. At some point the doorkeeper asked Peter an innocent question regarding his relationship with Jesus; this led to Peter's infamous triple denial. We have not been specifically told the high priest's connection to John, but he appeared to be bolder than Peter as Peter slipped out, a dejected and sorrowful man.[3]

Crucifixion and resurrection

John buttressed his personal devotion to Jesus by mentioning himself as the only one of the twelve to witness the crucifixion. Also, John presented his trust treaty with Jesus in these words, "When Jesus therefore saw his mother and the disciple standing by whom he loved, he said unto his mother, 'Woman, behold your son,' then said he to the disciple, 'behold your mother.' And from that hour that disciple took her into his own home" (John 19: 26–27). No doubt John considered this the greatest of his honors as he received the seal of the love of Jesus. There was speculation that John was related to Mary's side of the family. *The Expositor's Greek Testament* concluded, "If Salome was Mary's sister, then Jesus and John were cousins, and the commendation of Mary to John's care is in part explained."[4] In any case, Jesus' entrusting His mother to John's care might cause one to ask two questions. Was John spiritually ready to accept changes in responsibility? Had he matured since the days of anger and prejudice? The answer must be a resounding yes.

John demonstrated even more spiritual growth at the resurrection in two examples that he recorded; both examples to some degree involved Peter. The first example was almost comical in nature. Peter and John were in a foot race to the tomb of Jesus, and John outran Peter. Then, John almost timidly deferred to Peter, who seemed to be the older and the leader and who entered the tomb first (John 20: 3–8). In this case John demonstrated a humility and gentleness that were to be his signature attributes for the rest of his life. The next example involved Peter's curious question regarding the future of John's life. In John 21:21, Peter asked Jesus, "What shall this man do?" Jesus told Peter that this was not his concern but to concentrate on his own life.

In his gospel, John portrayed himself as reticent in demeanor and a close confidant of his Lord. When one compares this picture with the other gospel accounts, one can only surmise an extraordinary bit of maturation on John's part during the latter months of the ministry of Jesus. At times he emerged as confident and trustworthy, and at other times he demonstrated respect and deference to Peter, the leader of the disciples. Perhaps John did not mention his brother James in his gospel out of sadness; James died early in life by the sword. Peter likely took the place of John's lost brother. We now turn to the years following the death of Jesus, the years in Jerusalem.

JOHN IN JERUSALEM

S ince John the Apostle lived a life of unusual length, the temptation is always present to try to trace that life from beginning to end. In truth we can only make generalizations about his youth, concentrate on the gospel accounts for his years with Jesus, and make educated speculation on John's years in Jerusalem. He was mentioned by Paul as being one of the pillars of the Jerusalem church at the council meeting of AD 50. Wescott believed John's gospel was written after the year AD 70. Wescott acknowledged that the "composition of the gospel must be placed late in the generation which followed the destruction of Jerusalem."[1]

Pillar in the Church of Jerusalem

Thus we have a period of time, between the years AD 32–33 to 70, in which John completed a spiritual odyssey and became a leader in the Jerusalem church, the great church of the first fifty years of the first century. During these years the gospel, as proclaimed by Paul and others, spread to the Gentiles and throughout the Roman Empire. As far as we can tell, John remained in or close to Jerusalem.

The reign of Caligula and Claudius

At this time world events were changing rapidly. The declining years of the reign of Tiberius were followed by the rule of Caligula from AD 37 to 41. During this period, he restored Herod Agrippa to favor, exiled Herod Antipas, and treated Herodias as the sister of his friend Agrippa and not as the wife of his enemy Antipas. Bruce commented that during this period Antipas' tetrarchy of Galilee and Peraea, with the rest of his property, was added to Agrippa's kingdom.[2] Caligula's rule was characterized by bouts of mental instability that included rash promotions of favorites and executions of those who disagreed with him. At one point Caligula wanted to appoint his horse as consul. Caligula's paranoia grew until the Praetorian Guard assassinated him.

At the time of his death Caligula was preparing to desecrate the temple in Jerusalem. His death thus relieved the Jewish people and ushered in a somewhat calmer period under the rule of Claudius. Tacitus had written about the deification of emperors beginning with Augustus including building temples and divine worship.[3] It would be hard to imagine this tradition continuing with regard to Claudius. He was pictured by Roman historians as a content bungler who somehow muddled through his reign. Luke did mention that Claudius banished Jews from Rome, but gave no reason. The writer Juvenal recorded the Roman problems with the Jews in his Third Satire: "Though now the Sacred Shades and Founts are hired by banished Jews, who their whole wealth can lay in a small basket or a wisp of hay."[4] Such social problems did not reach the Jews of Galilee during Claudius' rule, but financial problems were always present in certain locations because of famine.

Claudius ascended to imperial power at the mature age of fifty. Seutonius, who loved to mock Claudius, referred to his appointment of Felix as governor in Judea.[5] At this time the Herodian power line had been temporarily halted by the death of Herod Agrippa. Later historians have been somewhat kinder to Claudius, regarding him more competent than inept. At times he seemed to be an introspective scholar as he wrote twenty volumes of Etruscan history. Michael Grant wrote, "Although, for instance, his mind was seething with good ideas, he evidently found it hard to coordinate them in a concisely expressed form."[6] However, Claudius did offer the people of Israel some relief from the complete madness of Caligula.

While not directly linked to goings on in Rome, the Zealot population of Judea and Galilee became more active. Bruce stated that in the year AD 44 these two sections of Israel became the one province of Judea. Bruce made clear that only in that year did Galilee become part of Judea and "so directly subject to imperial rule."[7] This year was also the year Herod Agrippa and James, the brother of the Apostle John, died. Both deaths were recorded by Luke in the Book of Acts.

External forces were pressing full force on John. The loss of his brother would have been tremendous, yet he did not record this tragedy in his writings. The Zealots would have been completely opposed to the consolidation of Roman rule in Israel. The church must have been feeling pressure in Jerusalem. Herod Agrippa, before his death in year AD 44, had considered the church's growth to be a real threat. The influx of believers as recorded in Acts 2, and the merger of the Hebraic and Hellenistic Jews as recorded in Acts 6, distressed local Jewish religious leaders who exercised increasing influence on Agrippa to halt such growth. Hence the execution of James, John's brother, was ordered by Herod Agrippa. Persecution against preachers increased and, in one case recorded in Acts, led to death. The martyrdom of Stephen, as recorded in Acts 7, showed that the church was facing intense pressure. With these scenarios in mind, we will look closely at John and his preaching partner, Simon Peter.

ACTS AND BEYOND

The gospel writer Luke continued his history in the Acts of the Apostles. In so doing he carefully detailed the birth of the church and quickly asserted Peter and John as the main evangelists, the first missionary team. Thus began one of the great evangelistic partnerships of the New Testament and revealed yet another facet of John's personality. John played a secondary role, this time not to his brother, but to the great man of Pentecost, Simon Peter. The stage was set quickly with Peter's great sermon in Acts 2.

Peter and John

What has been often overlooked after Pentecost is Acts 3:1. "Now Peter and John went up together to the temple at the hour of prayer." Notice how far John had traveled spiritually from being the other brother or one of the sons of Zebedee. Great change had occurred since the fiery "Son of Thunder" wanted to eliminate the opponents of Jesus.

John's life had changed in many ways by the time Luke wrote the Book of Acts. Now, Jesus was viewed as a tender and loving savior. John had witnessed the crucifixion, the only one of the twelve, by the gospel accounts. He ran to an empty tomb. He was caring for the mother of Jesus. Still a young man, perhaps in his early 30s, John had matured in many ways and in a very short time. Peter must have noticed John's inner peace. John was chosen by Peter over the rest of the apostles to be his preaching brother, his alter ego, a calming influence for the trials that lay ahead.

This evangelist team entered the temple as recorded in Acts 3. According to Bruce, Peter and John were acting as "the leaders of the twelve." This John was certainly the one known as "the son of Zebedee."[1] Peter immediately demonstrated his leadership by his ministry of healing, beginning with a crippled man. He delivered a great sermon at the Colonnade of Solomon on the east side of the temple. Yet, it was John who remembered and recorded that familiar setting when he wrote about Jesus walking at the Feast of Dedication (John 10:23).

Luke documented the boldness of both Peter and John in Acts 4:13 when he wrote in a most quoted but little understood passage regarding the two that these men "were uneducated and untrained filling the leaders with amazement." Many sermons have been preached about this verse to attempt to prove that Peter and John were little more than uneducated bumpkins unable to complete a sentence, much less write one, and were thus somehow infused with a special Holy Spirit language.

While it is certainly true that their lives were filled with the Spirit, Peter and John were quite well-educated for their time and position. Bruce commented that "illiterate" was not the intended meaning in this verse and that Peter and John were accurately described as commoners, "not priests or religious scribes." Both had the education common to Jewish tradesmen and businessmen of their day. The conclusion, as supported by Bruce's observations, can only be that Peter and John were teaching with authority, and that God was using the power of two extremely intelligent, spirit-filled men to exercise His will in Jerusalem.[2]

Notice that where Peter had been the spokesman in the earlier chapters, Luke now recorded both men speaking with undaunted courage. In Acts 4:19 and 20, Peter and John explain, "Whether it is right in the sight of God to listen to you more than to God, you judge. For we cannot but speak the things which we have seen and heard." The transformation in John's life was complete. There was no turning back. His heart had already been without fear, and now his tongue expressed his witness for the Christ.

However, John was not considered as the leader of the Jerusalem church. Luke recorded Peter as the chief arbiter in the Ananias and Sapphira scandal recorded in Acts 5. In Acts 6, Peter and the apostles delegated the Hellenistic widow problem to a number of special servants, precursors of the deacons of later times. Among these servants were Stephen, a great orator who paid for his faith with his life, and Philip, who converted other Jews, including the Ethiopian noble. In Acts 10, it was Peter who was given the responsibility of converting a Roman centurion who became a symbol of the Gentile mission ahead.

In Acts 12, Luke focused on the trials and tribulations of Peter. John's brother James was mentioned in connection with his execution by Herod Antipas. John was not mentioned, but Peter's imprisonment was detailed extensively, including his miraculous release from prison. The church in Jerusalem prayed in the house of Mark, but John the Apostle was not specifically named.

The last historical date for John in the book of Acts was his presence at the Jerusalem council of AD 50. Luke recorded this event in detail in Acts 15. Paul also referred to the event in Galatians 2 where he named Peter and John as "pillars" in the Jerusalem church. Paul stated, "They gave me and Barnabas the right hand of fellowship that we should go to the Gentiles, and they to the circumcised. They desired only that we should remember the poor, the very thing which I was eager to do." Again, as in Acts 2:9 and 10, John did not hold a special leadership role but was counted as equal among the leaders of the Jerusalem church.

The reign of Nero and Vespasian

About this time in history, the Roman leadership was changing. Claudius had given way to Nero in AD 54, and the next fourteen years were to be especially violent for the church. Nero had little to do with the Jewish people except for the appointment of Festus who showed some consideration to Paul when he was in prison. Through recent research, we have learned that James, the half brother of Jesus, assumed the primary post of leader in the Jerusalem church.

Bruce has made the assumption that this James appeared not to have traveled much though Peter and John traveled quite extensively.[3] In his various articles for *Biblical Archaeological Review*, Herschel Shanks concluded that this same James was the leader of the Jerusalem church at the time of the council of AD 50 and that his decree for the Jews to accept the Gentiles, not to impose dietary laws but to prohibit idolatry in any form, helped to cement relations between Paul and the other apostles. Shanks concluded that the resurrection of Jesus, sealed with a personal appearance, persuaded James to accept Jesus as Christ.[4]

Certainly Acts did not speculate on the relationship of the "pillars." In fact Peter and John were not even mentioned after the fifteenth chapter. Luke ended his history with Paul arriving at Rome in the year AD 55, thus a gap that cannot be documented by scripture. Tradition stated Peter traveled to Rome where he was executed during the reign of Nero. There has been little evidence that John left Jerusalem before the 60s. A significant event occurred in AD 62 when James, the leader of the Jerusalem church, was murdered by certain religious authorities. Another historical date, AD 70, was a watershed event in Jewish history. The Jewish temple was destroyed during the siege by the Romans. This disaster caused the great dispersion of the Jewish population including the Jewish church. Acts did not mention these events or the global changes occurring at the same time.

By the year AD 66, Nero's reign reflected his deteriorating personality. Michael Grant mentioned an abortive attempt by Nero's entourage to murder the emperor in the Circus Maximus. Among those arrested and executed were Seneca, the philosopher who was Nero's personal mentor, Lucan the poet, and Claudia Antonia, the daughter of the former emperor Claudius. Grant surmised that in that year "there were constant suspicions and alarms of further plots."[5]

Nero, as emperors before and after, had begun his reign with the best of intentions but in later years completely lost touch with his political situation. He had become much more interested in his theatrical accomplishments and his performances in chariot races. Seutonius wrote of his being "carried away by a craze for popularity."[6] Grant stated that Nero became "too bemused by his artistic career, to treat the empire as a serious full-time job, Nero had lost touch with hard realities, and paid the penalty."[7] With few allies left, he fled Rome and was assisted in suicide in AD 68 by a servant to spare him from being captured alive. To the end Nero maintained his belief that he was an artist, "*qualis artifex pereo*" (what an artist dies).[8]

In the year following Nero's death, the empire was to endure the short reigns of three emperors, all of which were over by AD 69. The fourth emperor after Nero, Vespasian, survived and restored a semblance of order. His credentials were well-known. His mission was to bring Roman authority where local governors had failed. Karen Armstrong, a religious historian, observed that beginning in AD 60 Rome had appointed men of "lesser caliber as Governors of Judea."[9] These appointments included Alibinus and Florus who proved to be disasters. As mentioned, the year 62 was the year that James, the leader of the church in Jerusalem, was martyred. This event presaged further unrest and eventual anarchy. The Jerusalem church must have suffered greatly. Armstrong reminded us that Rome sent its ablest general to quench the Jewish revolt.[10] By the year 70, under the direction of General Titus, the son of Vespasian, the Jewish revolt was crushed. With the temple destroyed, Jewish life was changed forever.

Closing years in Jerusalem

During these years where was John the Apostle? Before Paul left for Rome in the 50s, he mentioned his gift to the Jerusalem church. Apparently the church there had fallen on hard times financially. As far as we know the Jerusalem church did not assist Paul in his captivity either in Jerusalem or Caesarea. The warning of an assassination attempt came by way of his nephew who may have been a member of the Jerusalem *ekklesia* or church fellowship. Paul was forced to rely on his Roman citizenship for protection. Peter, John, and James apparently did not visit him while he was in prison at Caesarea. The cause might have been avoiding persecution, but the fact remained Paul and his party and the Jerusalem church had little alliance during this period.

The state of the Jerusalem church remained much in question even after the relief effort of the other churches. Even if fellowship remained with other churches, the demographics were changing. Eusebius, a church historian, observed that the apostles in Jerusalem, being "harassed in innumerable ways, with a view to destroy them, and driven from the land of Judea, had gone forth to preach the gospel to all nations, relying upon the aid of Christ."[11] Eusebius wrote at length about the terrible sufferings of those remaining in Jerusalem and mentioned those who fled to Pella beyond the Jordan. Were Peter and John in this group? Again, we have no documented record that either Peter or John were still in the Judean region in the 60s or at the time of the destruction of Jerusalem in AD 70.

We can only conclude that during the years of Acts and beyond, John matured into a respected evangelist, having changed his attitudes toward Gentiles as seen in his preaching outside of Judea. Yet, he was still not the leader that Peter, Paul, or James, the brother of Jesus, had become. John was that steady figure in the Jerusalem church, one of the pillars by the year 55. His greatest years lay ahead in the city of Ephesus.

JOHN IN EPHESUS

The early years of Christianity demonstrated different viewpoints. Peter, John the Apostle, and James, the brother of Jesus, stayed in Jerusalem or close by. On the other hand, Paul began his first of many trips to the Gentile world beginning in the 40s and continuing until his death before the year 70.

The dispersion

James was the great influence in the Jerusalem church, even more than Peter. Paul and James brokered a compromise in the year 50 at the Jerusalem conference. However, Paul saw that Peter and even Barnabas, his close friend and fellow missionary, continued to hold to Jewish traditions even after the conference. Paul confronted Peter after the latter had refused to eat with Gentiles at the common table while in Antioch. Paul recognized the influence of James and the Jerusalem church in this affair and so states in Galatians 2.

We can conclude that John was witness to these discussions and maintained a fondness for teaching his Jewish brethren as did Peter and James. Undoubtedly, John felt the intense pressure of the problems pressing in on the Jerusalem church as that entire region did. He also had the added care of the mother of Jesus.

Did John continue to care for Mary after James became a believer, or did James and other family members assume more responsibility? These are questions that cannot be completely answered because they are not addressed by any of the first century writers. There can be no doubt that John gained from Mary even more insight into the life of Jesus; John's gospel reflects this insight.

Douglas Moo in his commentary on the letter of James noted the effect of the Judean dispersion, which initially began with the stoning of Stephen, upon the Jerusalem church. Moo wrote about the severe economic disturbances, including the famine in Judea in the year 46 recorded in Acts 11:28, and the beginning of the serious social, political, and religious "upheavals that would culminate in the Jewish war of 66–70."[1]

John goes to Ephesus

Most scholars have agreed that John the Apostle spent his later years in Ephesus. We can place his final years at about AD 98–100. We also can project that John, as well as Peter, left Jerusalem before or in the year 70. Then there is the question of why John would move to this particular city, Ephesus. One ancient tradition speculated that Mary, the mother of Jesus, had died, and John was no longer under the obligation of providing for her care.

John, although reared in a small town, had become a city dweller. Wayne Meeks wrote that "Paul was a city person."[2] The same could eventually be said about John. Although we are not told the extension of his mission efforts with Peter, we can accurately predict that their travels included Asia Minor and thus Ephesus. Peter later addressed his letter to Christians in Asia Minor. John in his later writings included the cities of Asia Minor.

The history of Ephesus

Ephesus had long been the jewel of Asia Minor and would continue to be so for many years after the death of John. In about 500 BC, the philosopher Heraclitus flourished there. Heraclitus has been best known for his belief that the only constant in life is change, illustrated by the fact that one cannot step into the same river twice. He was also known for his belief in the *Logos*, a principle to which John gave a great deal of religious value. According to G.T.W. Patrick, "By the *Logos* of Heraclitus was indicated Law, Truth, Wisdom, Reason."[3] Other historians and philosophers agree about Heraclitus. Rex Warner adds, "He seems to have written his work about 500 BC, and is said, instead of publishing it, to have deposited it in the temple of Artemis in his native city." Warner observes, "His style is prophetic and even in antiquity he was known as the Dark."[4] Frederick Copleston also found the concept of the *Logos* in the writings of Heraclitus. Copleston concluded from Heraclitus that "man's reason is a moment in this universal Reason; and man should therefore strive to attain to the viewpoint of reason, realizing the unity of all things and the reign of unalterable law."[5] From the very beginning Ephesus was a center of philosophical thinking with the concept of the *Logos* well in place. We now will turn to later history.

Bourbon in his book about lost civilizations wrote that the ruins of Ephesus "still reveal the wealth and luxury, the intense trading and other business, the brilliant cultural life of this ancient Ionian city which flourished from the 6th century BC onward with various governments and political influences including oligarchies, tyrannies, Persian satraps, democratic colleges, Hellenistic dynasties, and Roman governors."[6] The great temple of Artemis was built about 550 BC. Another of the great buildings of Ephesus was the theatre with a seating capacity of 24,000.

These wonders placed Ephesus as a leading city of the ancient world. In his book about Greece and Rome, Meyer Reinhold took note of the increased Persian influence beginning with Cyrus in 550 BC and extending until the time of Alexander the Great. Reinhold wrote, "Among the areas the Persians conquered and annexed were Lydia, the Ionian Greek cities, Egypt, and the entire Middle East as far as sections of Western India."[7] Reinhold called this the Persian peace.

In truth Ephesus always seemed to have an oriental influence. Peter Green in his book about ancient Greece showed the picture of a high priest that he described as a "Greek work showing oriental influence" that was found in Ephesus about 700 BC. Green wrote that the Persian peace was influential in the Ionian region during the time of the Greek revolt in 480 BC. He concluded that in Ionia the rich coastal cities such as Ephesus and Miletus enjoyed forty prosperous years of Persian rule before raising a banner of revolt.[8] After the defeat of the Persians by the Greeks, Ephesus was prized by both the Athenian and Spartan leagues during the Peloponnesian wars. Thucydides related the sacrifices made to Artemis during the war against the Persians and documented that Themistocles, the Athenian general, sailed to Ephesus and then journeyed inland with one of the coastal Persians and "sent a letter to King Artaxerxes, Xerxes son, who had just come to the throne."[9]

The importance of Ephesus as a port city continued into both the Hellenistic and Roman periods. Michael Grant recognized it as a provincial harbor that received Roman exports. He also credited Ephesus with being a university town, less than Athens, but one of the other Greek centers of learning "such as Tarsus or Alexandria."[10] Indeed, Paul quickly recognized both these advantages while lecturing at the school of Tyrannus and meeting with Ephesian elders at Miletus. Peter Green stated that while in Asia Minor even Alexander the Great spent most of his time in Ephesus "because of administrative duties."[11]

Thucydides had remarked that though Ephesus had been a center of struggle between Athens and Sparta, the citizens of Ephesus had continued to hold festivals honoring athletics and literature. Likewise, from the Persian war through the period of Alexander the Great and his heirs, the Seleucids, the influence of Ephesus, continued as a city of commerce and learning largely because of its strategic location. Grant considered it the gateway of the Eastern provinces. By the time of Augustus, Ephesus was a great city to be ranked with Athens, Alexandria, and Antioch. The citizens were assured the equanimity of the reign of Augustus, and as Tacitus remarked, "Nobody had any immediate worries as long as Augustus retained his physical powers, and kept himself going."[12]

This city continued its importance into the period of the apostles. The populace had overwhelmingly kept allegiance to Greek and Roman rule. Alexander had found the people receptive as did Augustus. The city honored Augustus as a divine Caesar. A.R. Burns wrote that Ephesus with its Ionian traditions was a "progressive region of the Greek world." He brought out a well-known fact, that the Ephesians were of a mystical nature while they also combined the logic of the philosopher Heraclitus.[13]

The question was not so much why John eventually found a home in Ephesus, but how could he not be drawn to such a great center of learning, both religious and secular. The combination of the logic of Heraclitus with the ancient devotion to Artemis or Diana, to the mixture of eastern and western beliefs proved an irresistible challenge to the curious soul of John. Here he was to spend the last twenty years of his life.

The New Testament writers frequently included Ephesus in their writings. In the book of Acts, Luke introduced us to Paul's Ephesus. In the eighteenth, nineteenth, and twentieth chapters of this book, we can glimpse into the city that, at a later time, John would call home. Paul entered the city after leaving Greece and went to the synagogue, his usual place for presenting the gospel message. With Paul were two of his closest friends, Aquila and Priscilla, the wonderful husband and wife missionary team. Among their other accomplishments, they succeeded in improving the knowledge of the great preacher Apollos.

After quick trips to Caesarea, Jerusalem, and Antioch, Paul returned to Ephesus where he stayed for at least three years. Bruce described the Ephesians of this time as extremely devoted to Artemis, the local goddess. Her statue was housed in a great temple in the city. The Ephesians had changed the image of Artemis or Diana, the Roman name, from the ancient huntress of Greece to the fertility goddess of Asia. Bruce wrote that at this time the city prided itself as the temple warden of Artemis, and the cult of the great goddess had spread out into the whole "Greek world and even beyond its frontiers." He added that the temple was an amazing four times the size of the Athenian Parthenon.[14]

As mentioned, while in this great city, Paul lectured at the school of Tyrannus and must have encountered the city's intense interest in magical writings and spells. It seemed that the Ephesians tried to balance their Greek philosophy, as symbolized by the lecture halls of this school, with oriental magical inscriptions. Even the Jewish populace had succumbed to these esoteric spells and some, the seven sons of Sceva mentioned by Luke in Acts, had unsuccessfully attempted an exorcism in the name of Jesus. Bruce maintained that the greatest attraction of Ephesus during Paul's time was the great commercial interest, especially in regard to the worship of Artemis. The crafty Ephesians had made the worship of Artemis a lucrative business. Bruce wrote, "The success of Paul's evangelistic activity meant a diminution in the number of worshippers of the great goddess Artemis, and a consequent diminution in the income of those craftsmen who depended heavily on the Artemis cult for the sale of their wares."[15]

Paul escaped Ephesus with his life thanks to Roman law being exercised by the town clerk and some Jewish friends who wanted no part of an Artemis riot that could have developed into anti-Semitism. Following the efforts of Paul's mission to Ephesus, a successful church in that area began. In fact, these evangelistic efforts were one of the most fruitful phases of his career. Paul had established a church that would later welcome John the Apostle into its assembly. Thus John would find a city with a strong religious and philosophical background, a city that was the leading commercial city of Asia Minor, a rich city with a diverse population, and a city where East met West. This is the Ephesus that, upon his arrival around 70 AD, John was to call home.

However, what we know about John in Ephesus is beyond the province of scripture. We know from ancient writings that John was considered a respected elder in the church. *Elder* was used in the term of older person as by this time John was considered an old man. Most people in this period of history did not live to age fifty; John was already nearly seventy. Because of the length of his life, his legendary status grew as he became the last link to the ministry of Jesus. It was almost as if he had been rescued by God from an early death to inspire future Christians.

B.F. Westcott wrote that nothing is better attested in early church history "than the residence and work" of John at Ephesus.[16] Westcott reminded us that the dates of the beginning of the residence and its close are unknown. He was certain, however, that the work began after the departure of Paul and lasted till the close of the century. A memory came from Ireneaus, an early church leader, who told the story that John refused to enter a public bath as long as a certain heretic was in the building. Westcott rendered John's words as, "Let us fly lest the bath fall on us, since Cerinthus is within, the enemy of the truth." Westcott also recalled that Clement of Alexandria, another early church leader, mentioned John in extreme old age being carried by fellow Christians to the assembly repeating the command of Jesus "to love one another."[17]

John survived to be the last apostle. According to history, Peter and Paul were executed in the late 60s. From all accounts, Paul was martyred on the road to Ostia outside of Rome. The place of death for Peter has been less clear. But John, by surviving, became the foremost church leader for the remainder of the century. In his commentary on the gospel of John, Godet devoted an entire section to John in Asia Minor. Godet agreed with Westcott that John settled in Ephesus after AD 70, the date of the destruction of Jerusalem. Godet explained that the church's center of power had changed from Judea to outlying regions of the dispersion such as the seven churches of Asia Minor. He suggested that, after Paul's death, John filled the vacuum left in the region. Godet stated that as one of the last survivors John supplied a need for this region and watered "as Apollos had formerly done in Corinth that which Paul had planted." Godet concluded that John was the last link of Christ's church in the first century to Christ himself. In so being John joined the "heterogeneous elements of which the church had been formed."[18]

Godet added his name to those who believed that John lived to an extremely old age and remained unmarried (parthenios). Celibacy at that time was optional, practiced by some believers but as in the cases of Peter and James, the brother of Jesus, not practiced as both were married. Godet attempted to calculate John's longevity by mentioning that Irenaeus and Jerome, early church leaders, placed the time of John's death during the rule of Trajan which began in AD 98. Godet believed John to be about ninety to ninety-five years of age by this time. "He might have been in personal relations with the Polycarps and the Papiases who were born about the year AD 70."[19] John was born somewhere about the beginning of the Christian calendar and died very close to the year AD 100.

In his last years of life, John suffered persecution. Among the early church writers commenting on those years was Eusebius, mentioned previously, who was a very reliable historian. He was known as Eusebius

Pamphilos and was titled as Bishop of Caesarea in Palestine where he wrote his church history in the fourth century AD. His history covered the first three centuries of the history of the Christian community and ended with the ascent of Constantine as the Roman Emperor.

Because of his proximity to the time of John, Eusebius was in a prime position to know the events of the apostle's last years. He mentions the persecution of John by Domitian, the Roman Emperor, and John's exile to the island of Patmos in the Aegean Sea. Eusebius elaborates, "But after Domitian had reigned fifteen years, and Nerva succeeded to the government, the Roman senate decreed, that the honors of Domitian should be revoked, and that those who had been unjustly expelled, should return to their homes, and have their goods restored." Eusebius added that "the Apostle John returned from his banishment in Patmos, and took up his abode at Ephesus, according to an ancient tradition of the church."[20] These statements have helped to validate the year AD 96, which was the last year of Domitian's rule, as John's return to Ephesus.

Eusebius also referred to Clement's account of the travels of John around Asia Minor, after his return from Patmos. These travels included the appointing of bishops or elders and ministers and the encouragement of new congregations.[21] He recorded that John remained active in the life of the church as long as he lived. We may conclude from these writings that John's life remained remarkable both in quality and quantity.[22]

Finally in his classic work about Paul's missionary trips, William Ramsay also knew the importance of the Asia Minor region, particularly Ephesus. He wrote that Ephesus had been chosen by church leaders because of the seat of government there. He attributed the growth of the church in Ephesus in large part to its strategic location. Ephesus was on the main highway connecting the eastern regions of Antioch with the western regions of Rome, Athens, and Corinth. As Ramsay stated, "The great cities of Asia were on the highway of the world."[23]

As late as the middle of the second century, the emperor Verus met his bride at Ephesus.[24] This was the world where John lived and was to write, and with the support of the elders of the region John was able to turn to his writing. John was not like the Roman emperor Hadrian who traveled extensively over the known world to visit his subjects.[25] He was content to do his work in his special region. Now his writings must be examined.

THE GOSPEL

J ohn, as has been mentioned, would have found Ephesus a suitable place to write. He had been schooled in the Greek language as were the Jewish artisans and tradesmen. J.W. Roberts, in his commentary on the Letter of James, observed that it was well-known "that there was a deep penetration of Greek influence into Palestine affecting Galilee especially."[1]

The last gospel

The first book associated with John was his gospel narrative. In his commentary on this gospel, Frank Pack made the statement that it was unanimous among the scholars of the late second century that "John, brother of James and son of Zebedee, wrote the gospel in his old age while living at Ephesus." Pack noted that the internal evidence of this gospel overwhelmingly points to John the Apostle as the writer. This included a multitude of details that only an eyewitness could know, including the geography and topography of Israel; the attitude of the Jewish male population there toward women; the times and specific locations of feasts; the weariness of Jesus at the well of Jacob; the five loaves in the multiplication miracle being identified as barley loaves; the number of water pots in the house at Cana given as six; the number of fish, 153, caught by the disciples when Jesus prepared breakfast on the shore; and the identification by name of the high priest's servant whose ear Peter cut off. Pack concluded that "these details and many others come from one who saw and bore witness to them."[2]

The doctrine of the logos

The question arises, why another gospel? The so-called synoptic gospels had been written. Was the story of Jesus not completely told? According to John, there was a need for a special story about Jesus from not only an eyewitness, but from one who had a unique perspective. "In the beginning was the Word and the Word was with God and the Word was God. The same was in the beginning with God. All things were made by Him and without Him was not anything made that was made. In Him was life and the life was the light of men. And this life shineth in the darkness and the darkness comprehended it not. And the Word became flesh and dwelt among us, and we beheld his glory, the glory as of the only begotten of the Father, full of grace and truth" (John 1). From passages like this the reader immediately can notice that this gospel is different. The stories are different in content with much more detail. There is a great emphasis on the last days of the life of Jesus. And of course, there is the word transliterated *logos.*

The use of the Greek word "*logos*" has been the object of intensive and exhaustive research. Westcott thought that "the Word before the Incarnation, was the one source of the many divine words; and Christ the Word Incarnate is Himself the Gospel."[3] Pack suggested that the word was an attention getter for "Hellenistic Greek readers."[4] *Logos* can easily be translated as reason or logic. The English translates it simply as *word* which remains insufficient.

The *logos* doctrine defined this gospel as the word *grace* defined Romans. The first eighteen verses have been called the prologue in which John used the creation theme, a theme especially familiar to Jewish readers. In John's gospel, time was erased and Jesus became the eternal creator of the universe. John plainly stated that Jesus is part of the Godhead. He was not created, yet mystery of the ages, He came to earth in human form.

The main thrust of the prologue became the difficult and at times unfathomable concept of the immortal becoming mortal, the eternal creator living with the created. To John this meant life overcoming death,

Logos → The Word is God.

t dispelling darkness. If John meant for this relationship of light and darkness to represent good destroying moral evil, Godet concluded Jesus brought holiness together with the inward clearness, "the general intuition of the truth which arises from a good will."[5] We have by John's account the eternal deity living among darkness spreading the holy light of His presence. For each one of us no more profound passage of scripture exists. The Word or Logos becomes flesh and is the rationale for our faith and our hope. This passage becomes our eternal day of spring.

Dialogues

John, more than any other gospel writer, concentrated on the dialogues of Jesus. Three of these dialogues, or lengthy conversations, are in the opening chapters. John first remembered a certain wedding feast where he was present with Jesus, the disciples, and the mother of Jesus. The wedding occurred at Cana, near Nazareth, and was the most personal of the conversations since family members were involved. John was surely a witness and probably obtained details from Mary herself. Since these Jewish weddings lasted for days, disasters could and often happened. John remembered that when Jesus considered the predicament of the wine, He reluctantly remedied the situation with His first miracle. Jesus performed miracles only when there was a special need and certainly not at every distressful situation; He was very unlike the public charlatans of that day or of more modern times who exploited the helpless. Because of this, the Jews realized that His ministry was not one of miracles made to impress; Jesus did not heal everyone nor raise the dead in every village.

The first miracle of Jesus was remembered by John as the special request of Mary. This miracle, as related by John, demonstrated that Mary had already sensed the extraordinary power of her son. Jesus, she also knew, was struggling with the use of that power. Was a lack of wine at a wedding feast a suitable crisis for the use of His power? John concluded that

Mary knew Jesus was not only the healer of physical illness but the healer of social embarrassment. He was the Lord of healing and the Lord of joy. Jesus' human side was fully revealed at Cana when He saw the sadness and anxiety of the wedding party. John saw the details of the situation as no one else did.

Unfortunately the interpretation of this miracle has often concentrated on the alcoholic content of the wine, or on the seemingly harsh reply that Jesus made to His mother. The reason John recorded the miracle was because he wanted the world to see Jesus as a man of compassion, and a man interested in the joy of others. The original language showed that Jesus did not speak disrespectfully to His mother. He realized that the time had come to demonstrate His power.

Other lengthy dialogues were chosen by John for obvious reasons. Immediately, the reader can recognize the great contrast in the social standings of Nicodemus and the Samaritan woman, the people Jesus chose for conversations recorded in the third and fourth chapters of John. Nicodemus and the Samaritan woman were poles apart — one the epitome of the orthodox, respected, and at the top of the social strata — the other an outcast, racially and socially. Yet, John saw that both of them had a great desire for truth while harboring major deficiencies in their understanding of the Christ.

In the third chapter, John described Nicodemus as a ruler of the Jews. He came to Jesus by night, perhaps for his own safety as well as the safety of Jesus. Nicodemus had concluded that Jesus was a teacher from God and had recognized that Jesus could also perform miracles through the power of God. During their conversation, Jesus seized the opportunity to reveal the concept of spiritual rebirth. Nicodemus asked, "How can a man be born when he is old?" (John 3:4). Jesus answered that the birth was of water and spirit. Westcott wrote that water and spirit were part of the cosmic balance of the outward and the inward. He added that

Christian baptism, then and now, fulfilled the outward act of faith while the birth of the spirit sealed as well as united this outward act. The concept of the Spirit's action on the believer was compared to the mysterious ways of the wind. Westcott suggested that by word and deed through baptism the believer validated that an invisible influence had inspired and moved him.[6] Nicodemus finally admitted that he could not understand such teaching. As a symbol of the old order and the status quo, he could not grasp the new order of things. His world has been turned upside down by Jesus. *(really → upright—the way it should be!)*

Nicodemus believed that Jesus was a great teacher, but then Jesus said that He had been sent to earth as the unique Son of Man. Could Nicodemus believe this about Jesus? As Godet stressed, the Son of Man became the sole revealer of divine things, and Nicodemus was allowed to glimpse the heavenly secrets. Among these great secrets was the universal love of God through Christ. Nicodemus had not foreseen such revelations when he made his nightly appointment. He came knowing Jesus as a remarkable rabbi, but now he had been introduced to the teacher as the Savior of the World. Nicodemus now realized that he must experience a most radical change in his life. He could no longer regard Jesus as just another spiritual teacher. For this mature Pharisee, the night had become day, and the old had been replaced by the new.[7]

John chose another very personal dialogue to share a scene from Samaria. One can conclude that John was a witness as he was at Cana. This scene was quite different from the encounter with Nicodemus. As Luke had drawn the deep contrast in the Samaritan and the religious leaders, so John was saying that both the religious leaders and the outcasts of society needed Jesus. The dialogue with the woman of Samaria (John 4) began on a parched piece of land near the traditional site of Jacob's well.

In this remote area, Jesus saw none of the amenities of Hellenistic civilization. During this period of time the Roman world was replete with examples of this civilization as exhibited by the building programs started by Augustus and carried on by Tiberius. In such ruins as Pompeii, one is provided with a time capsule of first century life according to the Hellenic *Greek* and Roman way. At Pompeii, the remains of the theatre, the palestra, the baths, and the basilica still exist. As Salvatore Nappo observed, "Even the problems of the water supply were solved by the great aqueduct."[8] In Israel, Caesarea provided similar luxuries of the Roman experience. But at the well of Jacob, Jesus was far away from the civilized world.

John, who was to later live in Ephesus, was far removed from Jacob's well. In Ephesus John lived near the huge temple of Artemis that is described by Wayne Meeks as "one of the seven wonders of the world."[9] Even to the Jewish population of the first century, Samaria was considered the very dregs of the inhabited world. Perhaps only the wild province of Bithynia or the coasts of the North Atlantic could be worse. Jacob's well has been described by Jerome Murphy-O'Connor as "a deep well thirty five meters near Nablus."[10] Later, around about AD 380, a church was built there. The crusaders found the place to be a strategic location and built a new church on the spot in the twelfth century. Steven Runciman, the noted medieval scholar, recorded that Queen Melisandre lived in this exact region from 1152–1161 and that, as she grew older, she became "interested in pious works. She was known to found religious houses on a generous scale throughout her widowhood and made several grants of land to the church of the Holy Sepulcher in Jerusalem."[11]

In John the Apostle's time, Jesus was dealing with a Samaritan people that had some identity with the patriarch Jacob but were considered vastly inferior by both Judeans and Galileans. When Jesus met the Samaritan woman, she was very surprised to see a Jewish male ready to converse with her. Unlike Nicodemus, who valued his position as a religious leader and carefully came to Jesus at night, this woman was forced by her own society to come to the well in the middle of the day with its searing heat. This contrast of meeting times was emphasized by John.

Jesus created détente immediately when He asked for water from the well. This seemed a simple request by most standards, but by the mores of that time and place, the request was a complete surprise to the woman. Such hatred existed between Jews and Samaritans that the

woman was wary and began to list all of the barriers, such as you are a Jew, I am a Samaritan; you are male, I am female. John recognized later, perhaps by talking to the woman herself, that Jesus used this opportunity to move from the necessities of this life to the eternal verities. He told her about the gift of God; the gift of living water was discussed. The woman seemed to be theologically challenged, as was Nicodemus. She answered with a sense of unbelief while Nicodemus answered with more than a hint of skepticism.

After more exchanges in which Jesus revealed the secrets of her personal life, the woman acknowledged that He indeed was a prophet. Perhaps not so innocently, she changed the subject to a question about places of worship, as important in ancient times as it is in the modern world. As with Nicodemus, Jesus explained the new order of religious life, the spirit and truth concept. Then He chose the outcast woman of Samaria to make His great pronouncement that He was the Messiah. As Pack concluded, "To the Samaritan woman Jesus claimed first from his own life to be the promised Messiah for Samaritans, for Jews, and for all men."[12]

Miracles

Not only did John reflect on these dialogues, he also placed special emphasis on particular miracles of Jesus. The healing of the paralyzed man at the pool of Bethsaida (John 5:1–18) reinforced the concept of compassion in His miracles. John saw Jesus heal an obviously disabled person who had been ill for thirty-eight years as the author recorded in detail these years of illness, the inability of the man to reach the healing waters before the others, and the complaints of the religious leaders who wanted no healing on the Sabbath. The point was clear to John — neither God the Father, nor the Son Jesus rested from doing good works. As in the dialogues, Jesus was proclaiming a new order of life unfettered by the traditions of the past.

The healing of the blind man recorded in chapter 9 was John's natural progression into the complexity of the miracle process. The question was raised by His disciples as to who sinned. Pack enlightened us when he commented, "The rabbis held that the child could sin in the mother's womb. When a pregnant woman worshipped in a pagan temple, the unborn child also worshipped the idol. Also they held that the sins of the parents might be the reason for affliction."[13] Against such religious traditions, still to some degree present in more recent times, Jesus performed this miracle. John quickly realized that something was happening greater than the healing of physical sight. Jesus was taking on the great task of healing spiritual blindness that is always present in any age. He had come to wipe away the darkness of prejudice, misconception, and tradition. The blind man saw more than His critics and pronounced Jesus was from God. "If this man were not from God, He could do nothing" (John 9:33). John sadly saw that the healed man's reward for such perception was excommunication from the synagogue. The spiritual blindness of the world around him remained, and the spiritual leaders saw Jesus' truth least of all.

John recorded one miracle that stands on its own as both the greatest sign of the resurrection power of Jesus and also the most tender of His healing encounters. The story of His friend Lazarus has been simply called the resurrection miracle (John 11:1–44). John had recalled miracles relieving hunger and miracles relieving the suffering of the body; in the eleventh chapter, John presented the greatest of all the miracles of Jesus.

The family of Lazarus was very special to both Jesus and John. Their friendship was of the closest nature, and on several occasions this family provided Jesus and the disciples with an earthly home. Oddly, we have little knowledge of the family itself. Of the gospel writers, only John mentioned Lazarus. Luke mentioned the sisters, Mary and Martha, in Luke 10: 38–42 while showing their contrasting personalities. Mary was pictured as the intuitive one that was more admired. Martha was more pragmatic, busy with the order of the home. John described Lazarus in these words in the 11th chapter, "Now Jesus loved Martha and her sister and Lazarus."

The story simply told described Lazarus as very ill. Jesus seemed to delay going to him, and finally Lazarus died. Jesus then traveled to the family's home in Bethany where both sisters spoke freely to Jesus and told Him that their brother would not have died if He had come to Bethany sooner. In recalling this story in later years, John saw the plan that Jesus had for the situation; He would raise Lazarus from the dead four days after his death. As Jewish tradition observed, by the fourth day, the soul had ample time to leave the body. Both Martha and Mary recognized the extraordinary healing power of Jesus, but had not grasped His control of life and death. Perhaps they were not quite sure about the other raisings from the dead since they were done quickly after the person's death. Both sisters were grieving with a sense of hopelessness.

All of this, especially the sight of the vulnerable Mary, moved Jesus to His most caring moment in the gospel. Her genuine lament, as well as the lament of others, moved Him to tears. John at this point, above all the other gospel writers, merged the divine with the human in Christ. This miracle also displayed to John the complete submission of Jesus to the Father God. As Paul wrote in the Philippian letter, Jesus, even though of equal nature and stature with the Father, lived on earth as a submissive servant with complete submission to the Father. In this miracle, Jesus thanked His Father for hearing His prayer and allowing Him to demonstrate the glory of the one true God. Humility and submission were rare commodities in the religious world of that time as well as today. When Jesus had those standing at the tomb of Lazarus remove the stone, He showed mankind's proper submission to God's power. This resurrection was then completed with Jesus' loud voice in a command, "Lazarus, come out!" (John 11:43). John once again showed the simple way in which Jesus demonstrated the power of God. The completion of this miracle foretold the death of Jesus. From that moment on, He was considered a great danger to the religious authorities as well as the Roman government. John said that Jesus no longer traveled openly (John 11:54). Six days before Passover, He dined with the resurrected Lazarus for the last time (John 12:1).

Metaphors and models

John did not use parables as the other gospel writers. He did use the metaphors and models Jesus left. As a close observer, John recorded many scenes such as the anointing of Jesus at Bethany by Mary after the resurrection of her brother. The timing was spectacular. Lazarus was present at the dinner. Jesus was there in Bethany, the town that was so dear to Him. The closest friends of this special family were there. As usual Martha was serving as hostess. Mary realized her complete devotion to her Lord. The identity of Mary cannot be in dispute. In his careful way, John made a point to mention Lazarus and Martha. Only Mary, their sister who lived in Bethany, fit the profile. When Mary anointed the body of Jesus with an expensive ointment, she knew this was the proper thing to do. Marcus Dods in his commentary wrote, "This anointing was his true embalming. Mary's love was representative of the love of his intimate friends in whose loyal affection he was embalmed so that his memory could never die. The significance of the incident lies precisely in this, that Mary's action is the evidence that Jesus may now die, having already found an enduring place for himself in the regard of his friends."[14]

Mary's act of supreme devotion was significant to John because she blended the logical with the spontaneous. She must have calculated both the cost of the ointment and the time for the anointing. When she washed the feet of Jesus and dried them with her hair, John saw an act of supreme love and devotion. The act of unbinding the hair was not usually done by a Jewish woman in public. In a true sense she was unbinding her soul. How great was her devotion in contrast to the negative comments of those at the dinner. Judas Iscariot was one who camouflaged his greed by criticizing the act as wasteful, yet Jesus knew that Judas had impure motives while Mary was pure in heart.

In John 13 the writer presented his Lord as the model of service. John recorded events that had the most profound influence on him in later years. At this point he recalled an event that occurred during Passover week. Pack translated the pivotal verse in the present tense as the context dictates: Jesus rises from the table, lays aside his garments, and wraps a towel around him. Then he pours water into a basin and begins the process of washing the disciples' feet. The present tense emphasized that John could not forget the scene even many years later. The concept of service in rabbinic teaching never went to this extreme. Rabbinic teaching did not require even a Jewish slave to wash feet. Yet Jesus was always doing the unusual, touching the leper, exorcizing the demonized, eating with the tax collector, forgiving the sinful woman.[15]

Jesus had to tell Peter in a candid manner, "Unless I wash you, you have no part with me" (John 13:8). Peter then consented although he did not see the double meaning of cleansing. Jesus was foretelling His own sacrificial cleansing on the cross with His blood. He was also giving His disciples an example of life in service. The fourteenth and fifteenth verses of the chapter are climactic:"If I then, your Lord and Teacher, have washed your feet, you also ought to wash one another's feet. For I have given you an example that you should do as I have done to you." Pack interpreted, "Jesus had given them a supreme example, (*hupodeigma*), that applied to all their relationships to one another. The example of Jesus in this as in so many other things has been a most powerful incentive for devoted, sacrificial living and service among his followers."[16]

Another model of life was portrayed by John in the seventeenth chapter of his gospel. Jesus was shown praying His own prayer. After reading this prayer, a three part division can be seen. Jesus asked for His own glorification. In a cosmic sense Christ was following His own admonition to ask, seek, and knock. As in all of the requests of Jesus, He thought of His followers. He desired to give the ultimate gift, eternal life. John referred to eternal life in John 17:3 as knowledge of the only true God and His son Jesus Christ. In this case knowledge was more than rational consent but a complete bonding with God. Westcott commented, "It is not an acquaintance with facts as external, nor an intellectual conviction of their reality, but an apprehension of the truth by the whole nature of man."[17]

Jesus prayed for His followers to be protected. He was facing His own greatest crisis, but He thought of those who would be left. John had many years of life for which to be thankful. Perhaps in his later years he remembered Jesus' words, "Holy Father keep through thine own name those whom thou hast given me that they may be one as we are"(John 17:11). Protection came from God, but the third part of the prayer would be a choice made by each follower of Jesus.

Many have concluded that this prayer of Jesus was a call for unity. Certainly unity was a great consideration of Jesus, but protection from evil was an equal concern. John had lived long enough to know that the Evil One entered the heart of Christians to cause division. In a seeming contradiction of language, Jesus requested that His disciples not remain cloistered from the world, but at the same time, not participate in the world's beliefs. John knew the dangers of reclusive righteousness as well as the pitfalls of moral compromise. He never backed down from his beliefs from the time he was a young evangelist through the persecutions of the Emperor Domitian.

John could see that the prayer answered the requests for protection and unity by a call for a consecration of soul and a cleansing of spirit.

This complete consecration could, and still can, only be accomplished by adherence to truth. Truth here represented the full spectrum of God's revelations to humanity. These revelations were shown through natural forces of creation, revelations from the prophets of old, and finally through His Son. Westcott simply described it as "the sum of the Christian revelation."[18] Jesus was truly praying for future generations.

Many times the prayer has been used to implore unity of faith, but often the concluding verse has been forgotten: "And I have declared unto them thy name, and will declare it: that the love wherewith thou hast loved me may be in them, and I in them" (John 17:26). The definition of unity in these concluding words of the prayer has been interpreted in various ways. Pack wrote, "One of the strongest arguments confronting the world is the unity of Christ's followers based on his word."[19] Westcott expanded this unity in an almost esoteric aura: "Some mysterious mode which we cannot distinctly apprehend, a vital unity. In this sense it is the gospel of a higher type of life, in which each constituent being is a conscious element in the being of a vast whole."[20]

Both commentators are correct. Unity of believers has been based on the words of our Father. However, unity can never be achieved unless love is present. The divisiveness of the religious world has always had elements of contempt and bigotry. In the Middle Ages, crusading efforts often included massacre and pillage. The conquest of Jerusalem in 1099 by the crusaders was savage. Islamic forces then retaliated. Runciman's history of the crusades is filled with acts of brutality done in the name of religion.[21] Can anyone believe that Jesus prayed for such atrocities? Rather He prayed that the fellowship of believers be demonstrated by love—the love of the Father for the Son and the transmission of that love to all believers.

Thus, the very personal prayer of Jesus ended. It was a prayer as intense as any with the exception of the prayer in the Garden of

Gethsemane. Certainly, it has been a prayer for all the ages. The themes have continued to be universal in nature. John remembered this prayer, had pondered its contents all of his life, and revealed its glorious message for future generations.

John was the gospel writer who used many metaphors. In the picture of the good shepherd in John 10, Jesus told a familiar story to His listeners; He chose an occupation that was ordinary but familiar in the ancient world. The Jewish people could recall many good shepherds among their ancestors. Abraham had many flocks and herds; beloved David had spent his youth watching over his father's herds. Jesus may have had such illustrious shepherds in mind when He emphasized that the good shepherd would defend his sheep even to the point of risking his life. Abraham was forced into battle over his flocks, and David defended his sheep from wild animals. The key word was ownership. The good shepherd was not just doing his job, but he possessed the sheep and would never flee from them.

In a similar sense John was saying that Jesus owns us body and soul. The ownership was not one of natural possession but a personal relationship. John knew at this later time in history that Jesus, as the shepherd, not only would lead us but would protect us. John saw the great mass of believers as other sheep, and the message of Christ's love and protection would penetrate all barriers and extend throughout all generations. John described the story as a *paroimia,* a story similar to a parable, but with more of the mysterious. In any case the disciples did not understand the message any more easily than the more common parable. Jesus added to the metaphorical language by asserting that He was also the door through which the sheep enter safely. In returning to the thoughts of David in Psalm 23, Jesus became the fulfillment of the Lord as Shepherd. He became forever the provider for the needs of His disciples. He continuously set the table for His followers. He destroyed the fear of evil and accompanied His flock through the dangerous valleys. Goodness and mercy followed His own people, and they would enjoy His company always.

In chapter 15, John provided an even more intimate metaphor. Here Jesus referred to Himself as the vine and the disciples as the branches. Again as with the sheep, Jesus chose a most familiar scene. Then, as now, vineyards stretched from the Mount Carmel region down through Bethshemesh and the land of Samson. If one gazed at the vineyards with the grapes planted close to the ground, one would be reminded that a traveler in Israel could not miss the beautiful imagery of the vineyard. Pack stated that Israel was a land of vineyards, and the vine was associated with the "life of the people."[22]

John's emphasis in this metaphor was clearly the productive Christian life. However, that production cannot be separated from the Christian's connection with the source of all strength and beauty, Jesus Christ. Some interpretations associated the vine symbol with communion, but Jesus might not have had this specifically in mind. Certainly the Lord's Supper later came to be the ultimate symbol of the vine as well as the bread, but the imagery can stand apart from this reference. This metaphor extended to God the Father as the vine dresser. As Israel was the vine in the Old Testament, Jesus and His Father played these roles in the New Testament. God became the overseer. The productive branches of the vineyard were praised and became one with Christ; the unproductive ones were thrown away. When Paul wrote about the fruit of the spirit in Galatians 5:22, he was using a similar metaphor.

This metaphor extended the concept of the Christian's total reliance on Christ, not in the sense of protection as in the Good Shepherd, but in the realm of good works. Good works for the Christian were not a way to attach to Christ but rather were produced from the connection that was already there. We become bearers of good works through our total commitment to the grace shown by God (Ephesians 2: 8–10). We did not ourselves as branches in the vineyard but can grow and become fruitful through our love for Christ.

Another appealing metaphor that John related is found in the sixth chapter of his gospel. This metaphor was without question the most intimate of all. John contrasted the bread of life with the manna of the Old Testament. Again this passage has often been used in connection with communion, but John was obviously thinking far beyond that subject. To His audience Jesus presented His most radical teaching. To those who listened, the whole discourse about flesh and blood qualified as one of His hard or difficult sayings. John pointed out several eternal promises that his Lord made to those who would eat and drink; the cessation of spiritual hunger and thirst could be accomplished. John saw about him a deplorable spiritual famine. Only Jesus could provide spiritual nourishment. Jesus also promised acceptance to all those who would come to Him. How different from the message of exclusion that so many were hearing. Also, Jesus promised to become an inward part of all who were willing to put their trust in Him. How similar were His words to Paul's proclamation in Galatians that Christ lived within each Christian.

Westcott stated that the key verse of the chapter is verse 51 which was fulfilled in Christ's incarnation and resurrection: "By his incarnation and resurrection the ruin and death which sin brought in are overcome. The close of the earthly life, the end of the life which is, in one aspect, of self for self, opens wider relations of life."[23] Throughout the metaphor Jesus alluded to the Old Testament, in this case the manna of the wilderness wanderings. As in other comparisons, Jesus was pictured as the true and eternal, and the former is pictured as temporal. Manna sustained the people of Israel for only a brief period. It was a gift from heaven, and John did not discount that this bread was beneficial. John did point out, however, that manna was not the eternal bread of life; only Jesus provided the true *(alethes)* solution. As bread and drink are vital to this life,

Jesus is our spiritual bread and drink for the eternal life. The expansion of this metaphor came easily in the early church. The communion of bread and the fruit of the vine became integral in worship and served as a reminder to the participants of John's account where he witnessed the true Bread of Life.

The last week of Jesus

For John the defining period of time in his gospel was the last week of Christ's life on earth. More than any other gospel writer, he devoted his account to those last hours. Of all the gospel writers, only he witnessed the last supper, the farewells of service and prayer, the metaphor of the vine and branches, the betrayal, the trial, the crucifixion, and the resurrection. From chapters 13 through 21, John was our eyewitness, revealing to us the innermost secrets of Jesus.

After the Lord's prayer of protection and unity, John carried us to the scenes of the dark recesses of the Gethsemane Garden of the Kidron Valley. As one views the peaceful landscape today and the lush vegetation of the garden, one can hardly picture that dreadful scene found in John 18. Only John identified the man that Peter attempted to kill with his sword while defending Jesus. John contrasted the old order with the new as Jesus willingly sacrificed Himself while Peter fought. Jesus showed to the world the submissive nature that He would demonstrate even to the cross. John described the scene as one of total subjection of Jesus to the will of God the Father as the Son drank the cup that the Father had given Him. James Orr, in his article "Jesus Christ" contained in The *International Standard Bible Encyclopedia,* pictured the agony of Christ going beyond the horrible physical suffering to the realization of His dying for the sins of humanity.[24] John, who himself at times had shown an explosive reaction similar to Peter's, realized that one must not use the sword. Paul mentioned the submissive nature of Christ in the *kenosis* passage of Philippians 2 where Jesus emptied Himself of everything and became obedient even to "death on a cross" (Philippians 2:8).

After the scene in the garden, John quickly turned to the trial of Jesus. The inquisition before Annas and Caiaphas revealed a little known part of John's life. John and Peter followed Jesus to the palace of the high priest (John 18:15). However, only John entered the palace with Jesus as Peter stood outside in the courtyard. John described himself as the disciple who was known to the high priest (John 18: 15, 16). Westcott was aware of the tradition that John was privileged to wear the *petalon*, the plate attached to the high priest's headdress, the *mitre*.[25] Bernard went even further in his commentary when he stated, "We are inclined to accept the tradition that James, John, and Mark literally wore the petalon, at least occasionally, in virtue of their services as Jewish priests."[26] Thus, we can conclude that John, of all the disciples, had the credentials to enter the venue of the trial and report on the proceedings. Pack interpreted more when he recalled that early church tradition held that when John "was not at the temple serving as priest, he worked as a fisherman, and that John's family supplied fish for the high priest."[27]

The prestige of John's position allowed him to witness the tragic denial by Peter of Jesus in the courtyard. John identified one of the accusers of Peter as a "maid who kept the door" (John 18: 17). Godet reminded us that the "Hebrews very commonly had female doorkeepers."[28] This is also seen as Luke recorded the young girl who answered the door when Peter came to the house of John Mark (Acts: 12). John added to the validity of his witness when he recalled the charcoal fire that the servants had made (literally a heap of burning coals from which the English word *anthracite* comes). John used the same word when he later described the coals over which Jesus cooked fish (John 21:9).

John contrasted the drama of the examination of Jesus with the equally sad spectacle of Peter's denial. John, who must have known some of the priestly household, identified one of Peter's questioner's as a "kins-man of the man whose ear Peter had cut off" (John 18:26). John was also keenly aware of Jewish customs regarding Gentile courts. We can surmise that John filled the void left by other gospel writers in examining that Roman enigmatic figure, Pontius Pilate. In the eighteenth chapter of John, he pictured Pilate as baffled by the whole business. After all he did not see any real civil unrest perpetrated by Jesus Christ. Pilate remarked, "Am I a Jew? Your own nation and the chief priests have handed you over to me; what have you done?" (John 18:35). Later he issued his most con-troversial of statements, "What is Truth?" (John 18:38). In Pilate, John saw the great contrast in the spiritual government of Christ versus the cynical, pragmatic power of the Roman government.

In his final exchange with Jesus, Pilate chose to dismiss Him after he found that Jesus was more concerned with eternal matters than His own life. At that point Pilate had entered into the political labyrinth of compromise. He would release a known terrorist if Jesus was not freed. The angry mob frustrated this plan by choosing Barabbas the murderer. After more conversations with Jesus about earthly matters and heavenly concepts, Pilate presented Jesus to the accusers. The crowd accused Pilate as not being a friend of Caesar (*Caesaris Amicus*). Pilate caved in to politi-cal expediency. Pack summarized Pilate's position: "He might lose his governship, he might be summoned to account before the emperor him-self, and even suffer exile and public disgrace."[29] John saw Pilate as the ultimate display of the political, earthly mind. The man who told the crowd that he could find nothing wrong with Jesus joined the forces of evil through his inaction to save the innocent.

John was the only apostle at the crucifixion. He documented four women at the site. He did not dwell on the arduous walk of Jesus on the street called *Via Dolorosa*. No doubt he was there, but perhaps even late in life the memories were too painful. John did concentrate on Jesus as the fulfillment of the Old Testament as witnessed by him and others at the cross. The placard above the cross was mentioned only by John; it read "Jesus of Nazareth, the King of the Jews" in Aramaic, Latin, and Greek (John 19:19–20). John realized that Jesus represented sovereignty through suffering. The three languages were symbolic to John. Years later in writing his gospel, he comprehended that this crude sign was a symbol of all humanity.

Why in particular did John mention the four women at the cross? They were a diverse group and representative of that inscription above the cross. There was a great contrast between the mother of Jesus and Mary of Magdala. The first was chosen from all women to be the mother of the Son of God. The other was a recent follower of Jesus without the pedigree of other followers. Yet, both recognized Jesus as Lord. John's mother was also present, and she has been identified as the sister of Mary, the mother of Jesus. Perhaps John saw in these women at the cross a courage that the men did not have.

During the crucifixion, John was selected by Jesus to take care of Mary, His mother. Bernard wrote, "His dying eyes are fixed upon those who have been dearest. The forgiveness of enemies, the consolation of the fellow-sufferers; these give place to the thought of mother and of friend."[30] John, as always, was very careful to point out the human as well as the divine characteristics of Christ. He saw in these actions and sayings of Christ the fulfillment of prophecy such as the parting of His garments, the extreme thirst, and the bowl of vinegar. John's great attention to detail and his prodigious memory as he wrote the gospel molded the account into the most personal of experiences. His own emotions must have churned when he saw the Lord suffer as a human in the most horrible manner.

John saw the great symbolism. After the death of Jesus the soldiers had to test for any sign of life. The piercing of the side of Jesus was an act of brutality that John witnessed. On later reflection, he recognized that blood and water coming from the body were distinct symbols. Just as the inscription on the placard showed the world-wide validation of Christ's rule, the blood and water were complete symbols of His saving power. Westcott reminded us that for John blood "is the symbol of the natural life and so especially of life as sacrificed. Water is the symbol of the spiritual life; and Christ by dying provided for the outpouring of the Spirit."[31] John now understood the concept of the living water and the body and the blood that he later described in the third and the sixth chapters of the gospel. John summarized the death of Jesus with his personal testimony: "And he that saw it bare record, and his record is true" (John 19:35). "A bone of him shall not be broken, and they shall look on him whom they pierced "(John 19:36, 37).

The mood changed in John's gospel when he reached the climax of his account. He paid very special attention to the burial of Jesus. Ralph Gower wrote about the burial customs of the time saying, "The body was normally washed, wrapped loosely in a linen cloth, and carried to a burial place on a wooden stretcher. Burial could take place in a natural cave or an artificially made one. This was done for Jesus by two wealthy men."[32] John was verifying for all that the death of Jesus was real, and therefore the burial must take place. *The Expositor's Greek Testament* placed the validity of the death as John's priority even unto the piercing of the body: "It is not the phenomenon of the blood and water he so emphatically certifies, but the veritable death of Christ."[33]

John described two unlikely benefactors in the funeral arrangements. Joseph, who was of Arimathea, and Nicodemus, who was known as the ruler who came by night, prepared the body for burial. Both were members of the Sanhedrin, both were rich, especially Joseph, and both must have been profoundly changed by Jesus. Nicodemus was now bold in his faith in Christ. John must have reflected on the spiritual growth in this man since visiting Jesus at night. Joseph used his influence and wealth to properly care for the body including the providing of a garden tomb. Again, *The Expositor's Greek Testament* stated that "the Friday was so nearly at an end that they had not time to go to any distance, and therefore availed themselves of the neighboring tomb as a provisional, if not permanent place."[34]

One can almost sense the relief that John felt as these two noble men came with courage, much beyond the other disciples, to bury the Lord. John alone of the gospel writers remembered the exact weight of the spices used as well as the place of the tomb. Whether John assisted in the preparation for burial is unknown, but he was aware of so many details that such is possible, even probable. John had just experienced the most trying time of his life, a period he could never forget even fifty years later. This period of time had drained him emotionally and depressed him beyond words. Now, he was ready to present the glorified Christ.

At this point in the gospel, John remembered a woman who came to the garden alone. The other gospels mentioned women, but John featured Mary Magdalene. Only she had the courage to come to the tomb, and she came very early. (The other gospels indicated that other women came not too much later.) Mary then had the boldness to report the empty tomb to the disciples. John could not help but notice the fortitude of the women in contrast to the seclusion of the men. He mentioned that Mary knew where to find Peter. Westcott wrote that she came to a lodging place where Jesus' mother was staying.[35] The information following her report was given in the quintessential Johannine style.

Ever the stickler for details, John documented the foot race to the tomb. He reached the sepulcher first, but waited for his friend Peter, who entered the tomb first. When John entered the empty tomb, his life changed forever. Westcott concluded that, at this point, John separated himself from the other disciples. The agony of the garden burial, the cruelty of the cross, and the mystical references to resurrection began to make sense. John remembered the careful way in which the clothing was arranged. Nothing had been hurried. He saw the empty tomb and believed.[36]

When the resurrected Christ appeared to the disciples, John quickly noticed His physical and spiritual capabilities; this was the resurrection body. Jesus moved through closed doors and appeared and disappeared suddenly. Yet the resurrection body still contained traces of the human body. Jesus had fresh scars in His hands and His side. John's inclusion of the appearance to Thomas and his doubt was probably not so much for the benefit of the other disciples and certainly not to embarrass Thomas, but it was for future generations who had not yet seen and might never see the resurrected Christ. John recalled the special blessing of Christ on "those who have not seen and yet believe" (John 20:29). He then added a closing comment on his account: "Now Jesus did many other signs in the presence of the disciples which are not written in this book; but these were written that you may believe that Jesus is the Christ, the Son of God, and that believing you may have life in his name" (John 20:30, 31).

The closing chapter of the gospel related a breakfast scene by the sea. Here John was obviously an eyewitness. The story took the disciples back to their roots of fishing. After a fruitless night on the lake, the disciples thought they heard a stranger call out to them from the shore. He told them to cast out their nets on the other side of their boat; the result was that the disciples were unable to haul in the nets because of such a great quantity of fish, the total catch recorded as 153. John showed his intuitive nature when he recognized the first-supposed stranger as Jesus. Peter, always impetuous, jumped into the water and swam to shore. John then described what next took place. The disciples had been without hope. Now, they found Jesus cooking their breakfast, even asking them for a few of their fish.

Above all the story was not about the fish, but the reconciliation of Jesus with Peter. To John, Peter became the bedrock of the early church because of this reconciliation and forgiveness of Christ. His friend from the early days on the Sea of Galilee was now transformed into the leader of the Lord's church. John closed his message in triumph. Jesus had prevailed over death, and now Peter had overcome his fears.

John would have many years to ponder his own role. Why would he outlive the other twelve? As we look back through the centuries, we can see that John, of all the followers, was given the spiritual insight and sensitivity to write such a gospel. He alone could adequately describe the Word becoming flesh, Who lived, grew tired and thirsty, even cooked a morning meal for a group of men who had all but given up hope and purpose. John had changed from a son of thunder to a blessed apostle.

THE FIRST LETTER OF JOHN

"That which was from the beginning, which we have heard, which we have seen with our eyes, which we have looked upon, and our hands have handled, of the Word of life; for the life was manifested, and we have seen it, and bear witness, and show unto you that eternal life, which was from the Father, and was manifested unto us. That which we have seen and heard declare we unto you that ye also may have fellowship with us: and truly our fellowship is with the Father, and with his Son Jesus Christ. And these things write we unto you that your joy may be full." (1 John 1:1–4)

Place and authorship of the letters

The destruction of Jerusalem in AD 70 was in many respects a devastating blow from which the early church had great difficulty in overcoming. Nahum Agivad also viewed the utter destruction of the city to have this effect. In his description of the famous archaeological discovery known as "the burnt house" he wrote, "Soot reigned over all, clinging to everything. It covered the plastered walls, and even the faces of our workmen turned black. There was no doubt that the fire had rampaged here, apparently fed by some highly inflammable material contained in the rooms. It may well have been some oil, which could account for the abundance of soot. The traces were so vivid that one could about feel the heat and the smell of the fire. So at least some of our visitors mentioned. It was now quite clear that the building was razed by the Romans in AD 70, during the destruction of Jerusalem. For the first time in the history of excavations in the city, vivid and dear archaeological evidence of the burning of the city had come to light. We refrained from publicizing this fact immediately, in order to keep from being disturbed in our world by visitors. Something amazing occurred in the hearts of all who witnessed the progress of excavation here. The burning of the Temple and the destruction of Jerusalem—fateful events in the history of the Jewish People—suddenly took on a new and horrible significance."[1]

The excavation of Jerusalem and the findings surrounding its destruction were not the first unusual discoveries that had been made in archaeology. Hanns-Wolf Rachl recalled the unusual catch made by an Italian fisherman in 1832 when a bronze statue of Apollo was retrieved. He wrote, "Near the site of the find there once stood an ancient city, Populonium. The god, which today stands in the Salle des Bronces in the Louvre in Paris got caught in a fisherman's net."[2] And thus archaeology in some fashion has always shed light on ancient places. But in regards to our history of John, the verification of the destruction of Jerusalem was pivotal. Agivad noted that coins discovered in the burned house had no date later than AD 69.

By every indication John left Jerusalem either before the destruction of Jerusalem or no later than 70. He had probably written the gospel close to that year or a few years later. But what about the letters ascribed to him? The letters do not let us know the author directly. Irenaeus assigned the first two letters to John, the author of the gospel. Clement of Alexandria acknowledged that this same John wrote the first letter. Tertullian and Origen also acknowledged that John the Apostle wrote the first letter. The Muratorion Canon compiled in Rome between

AD 170 and 215 quoted from the compiler Hippolytes that John was the author of his gospel and these epistles. The commentator John R.W. Stott looked to the previous external evidence for assigning the letters to John the Apostle and contended that the internal evidence is just as strong. He wrote, "So far, then we have suggested that the similarities of subject matter, style and vocabulary in the Gospel and the first letter supply very strong evidence for identity of authorship, which is not materially weakened by the peculiarities of each of the differences of emphasis in the treatment of common themes. John is not teaching new truths or issuing new commands, it is the heretics who are the innovators. John's task is to recall them to what they already know and have."[3]

John most likely wrote his letters from Ephesus after he had left his roots of Judaism. He must have experienced both the fond memories of Jewish traditions in Jerusalem and the desire to proclaim the message of the Living Word among the dispersed Christians in Asia Minor. Gone were the days when he had his own home in Jerusalem, when he lived on the proceeds either of his fishing business or the kindness of brethren in Judea. Now he was in a Hellenistic city with Jewish and Asian influences. John was now considered an old man. With these thoughts the first letter can be addressed.

The introductory verses of this letter echoed the thoughts of his gospel. The emphasis now is more on the humanity of Christ, according to Lenski. He observed that there are four statements about Jesus. Two of these statements imply a continuous effect; what has been seen and what has been heard is remembered by John. Two other statements were simply statements of fact; John said that he and others saw the Lord, felt His flesh. He exposed the imaginations and delusions of the unbelievers.[4] John, as Paul does in Philippians, wrote about the eternal descent or *kenosis* of Jesus from the realms of heaven to a flesh and blood existence on earth.

The citizens of Asia Minor believed in gods descending, as they demonstrated in Acts, identifying Paul and Barnabas as Hermes and Zeus. They also considered that Augustus had been divine and worthy of a temple. John wasted no time in attacking the Christian perversion of idolatry when, as Stott phrased it, "this stress on the material manifestation of Christ to human ears, eyes and hands was of course directed primarily against the heretics who were troubling the church."[5] John was demonstrating the True God manifest in flesh and blood. John proceeded to develop his thoughts on lines that benefit the believers in the Word becoming flesh. Belief in Christ resulted in fellowship and joy. John was referring to the prayer of Jesus in John 17 that the believers be one. But was a complete fellowship in this life possible? The answer was no. Therefore, John was thinking beyond the relative happiness of earthly fellowship to a divine rapture of love that only heaven brings. Stott again observed that "consummated fellowship will bring completed joy, and

the eternal proclamation and historical manifestation of the Word will bring fellowship with one another, which is based on fellowship with the Father and Son and which issues in fullness of joy."[6]

Key words and Gnostic heresy

After his opening remarks, John wrote one of the key words of the letter, the word *light*. The Greek word was *phos* from which English derived many words such as *photography*. As Wuest wrote in his commentary, "The rule of Greek grammar is that the absence of the definite article shows quality, nature or essence and that God as a Person has a character or nature that partakes of light."[7] John used words such as light in the letters as he used metaphors in the gospel. Light became a key word in the battle against the Gnostic belief called antinomianism. This belief simply stated that manner of life made no difference to God. John countered this idea in verses six and seven of the first chapter: "If we say that we are having fellowship with Him and are walking in the darkness, we are lying and are not doing the truth; but if we are walking in the light as He is in the light we do have fellowship with one another, and the blood of Jesus, His Son, cleanses us from all sin." John defined light in reference to moral action. There were those in Ephesus who were influenced by Cerinthus, a leading Gnostic heretic. This situation recalled the problems that Paul faced in the Colossian church regarding Gnosticism.

The summary of this ethical heresy was that Christians had no real moral obligations as the body and the spirit could act independently. One could dwell in the darkness of a sinful life and still have fellowship with God. John repudiated this cheap grace with the statement that one can indeed be excluded from the sacred fellowship, the *koinonia,* of believers and is deemed a liar by God. As Lenski commented, "John does not speak of a communion of those who walk in darkness, who lie and do not the truth."[8] John further stated in verse 9 that all Christians must admit that their lives are not perfect for only then can the blood of Christ continuously cleanse their sins. The tense of the Greek verb implied that the cleansing is an ongoing action and occurred every minute of the Christian's life.

The real test of love can be found in the second chapter of this letter. John knew that the false intellectualism of the Gnostic belief excluded love for the brethren. In verse nine of the chapter, he stated that the one who "hates his brother is in the darkness." Another test of love was found in the attitude toward possessions. In many cases Gnosticism advocated a love of pleasure and drew sharp distinctions between the material and the spiritual. John was not advising people to abandon material possessions, but to remember the greater influence of the spiritual life. Certain possessions can be wrong, whether that be trust in intellectual power or the trust of material gain. True love (*agape*) avoided personal disdain for others and false hope in material matters. Although John had been successful in the trade of a fisherman, he did not make that his supreme goal in life. He was not advocating ascetic behavior nor was he advocating materialism. He was testing Christians in regards to their true love, the love of Christ and the love of the brethren.

John turned next to another Gnostic heresy. The Gnostics were denying the humanity of Christ, and thus they were antichrists. The last hour in 1 John 2:18 refers to the last epoch of time. Ross in his commentary wrote, "It is important to remember that according to the N.T., with the coming of Christ, with His Death and Resurrection and Ascension, the last period of the world's history has begun. God has spoken His final message in His son."[9] John could see that heretics like Cerinthus only validated the signs of things to come. Those who were, are, and would be Christians experience the evil enticements of the antichrist philosophy. John saw that these Gnostic beliefs might never leave the world, and he believed that Christians were all his little children who could and would be tempted by false teachers. Wuest observed that these children "must not allow themselves to become entangled in the Gnostic heresy regarding the Person of the Word Jesus."[10]

In the last part of the second chapter, John advised his listeners how to avoid such heresy. He admonished them to cling to the message that they had heard from the very beginning. As Stott remarked about those who are obsessed with the latest ideas, they "show themselves to be Athenian not the Christian." John further emphasized the great assistance of the Spirit who would indwell the Christian. This was the Spirit who, even today, will serve as the believer's personal advocate or *paraclete*, who will plead our case to God, and will interpret our innermost expressions of need (Romans 8). Stott presented the balance that the Christian must have in relying on the Holy Spirit as found in the scriptures.[11] We must remember that the Holy Spirit in John's teachings, as well as all writers of the New Testament, did not contradict the teachings of the gospel message in the scriptures. The Spirit would help each Christian when he prayed to Christ for protection. The Spirit would interpret petitions, and He would serve as advocate and protector. Still today, when teachings such as the ones fostered by the Gnostics come, the child of God will be protected.

In chapter three of his first letter, John considered the Christian's present and future existence. John, as other New Testament writers, saw only two types of existence for the Christian, the flesh and blood of this world, and the exalted state of the next world. Unlike Eastern religions, there were no endless repetitions of earthly life, and unlike Gnostic beliefs, there were not any ladders of approach to heaven. John used the word *know* often to emphasize his certainty of future existence. He knew that great expectations were before the Christian. Ross defined John's attitude as feeling that the believer "shall be like Him, as He is now in His glory."[12] Greek society before Socrates believed in the divinity of the soul but had great difficulty with the concept of a glorified body. In

John's letter he believed that Christians would become as the glorified Lord. John was the last eyewitness to the resurrected Jesus. On the shores of Galilee, John had a glimpse of what Christians would become. Jesus had overcome death and ascended to heaven.

Wuest believed that John was talking about this physical likeness in the third chapter of the letter. Wuest was reminded of Paul's teaching in the third chapter of Philippians where the Christian's body will be changed from one of humiliation to one of glory: "We shall be like our Lord as to His physical, glorified body."[13] Stott contributed to the eternal discussion by leaning toward Paul's belief that, after death, the Christian will be in heaven with Christ. "It is enough for us to know that on the last day and through eternity we shall be both with Christ and like Christ, for the fuller revelation of what we are going to be we are content to wait."[14]

John did not explore this period between death and the *parousia,* or second coming. Paul referred to going to be with the Lord. Jesus gave the parable of the beggar in Abraham's bosom. In this letter John was more interested with the transformation in this world that constituted the beginning of an eternal relationship with God. He also addressed the nature of one's life in preparation for the next. John warned his readers that Christians could not remain in a lifestyle of sin. In this matter one had to directly confront the Gnostic heresy. As Ross so aptly worded it, "Sin is not in the believer the ruling principle, as it is in the case of the deficient persistent sinner."[15]

To emphasize the new life, the Christian not living a sinful existence, John provided a litmus test. Did the Christian love his or her fellow Christian? "For this is the message which you heard from the beginning that we should love one another; not as Cain was of the evil one, and slew his brother. And wherefore slew he him? Because his works were evil and his brother's righteous"(1 John 3:11–12). Ross portrayed the murder in this way, "The diabolical nature of Cain's crime came out in this, that it was his brother's righteousness and his acceptance with God that excited his murderous hate."[16]

The rest of the third chapter described the healing and transforming power of love to the Christian who chose not to live the life of sin. Again, John used the word *know*: "We know that we have passed from death to life, because we love our brothers. Anyone who does not love remains in death" (1 John 3:14). The Gnostic position was that knowledge alone solved life's problems, but this knowledge was available only to a select few. John was saying that true knowledge (*gnosis*) was demonstrated by true love (*agape*). John gave us the supreme example of love similar to Paul's illustration in Philippians, the second chapter. John concluded that if Jesus gave His life for us, we should be willing to give our lives for the brethren. This was a most dramatic example to be sure, and John then offered a more common example of the brethren in need. Lenski commented, "We are children of God when we show the evidence of love in deed and in truth."[17] This chapter thus ends the quest for a sinless life by admonishing the readers to love. Individual sins were recognized by John, and John rejected the Gnostic claim that one could not sin or that a lifetime of sin was acceptable. He further rejected the Gnostic belief that one could selectively love people. The child of God did not choose only the fellow intellectual as worthy of love or the person of wealth as worthy of grace. Love according to John was inclusive not exclusive, and was exhibited by deed as well as by word.

In chapter four John again emphasized what true belief is. Again the Gnostic heresy must be understood. The Gnostics did not believe in the sufficiency of Jesus as Lord nor did they believe in His humanity. In the Colossian letter Paul had to stress the completeness (*pleroma*) of Christ. Paul and John exalted Jesus as Lord rather than the Gnostic attitude of Jesus as simply one of the steps on the ladder to heaven. As a test of belief in Jesus as the Christ, John penned his ode to love in John 4:7–21. John stated that true love (*agape)* was shown by deed not just in thought.

John placed the crux of his argument with the origin of love: "Not that we loved God but that He loved us, and sent His Son to be the propitiation for our sins" (I John 4: 10). The emphasis was on God as the one initiating the deed, and the Christian as the receptor. God has always been the one who does the searching for the lost souls who hide from Him. Other verses in this chapter were essential to John's argument, including the thirteenth, where he wrote that "He has given us of His Spirit." The tone of this verse was assurance coupled with the evidence of God's love. Stott added, "By this we know that we live in him."[18] True belief produced love, and such pure knowledge, purged of the arrogance of contempt for others, assured believers of God's love and of the Spirit living within them.

Verse seventeen of this chapter taught the Christian to be assured to the point of boldness in the day of judgment. This day was described by Ross in many ways including "the last day; the day; and that day."[19] Lenski concluded, "If you still fear punishment from God, you have prevented his love for you from remitting your sins and thus from planting sure confidence in your heart."[20] Or as Stott commented, a Christian must continue his love of the individual for "it is easier to love and serve a visible human being, and thus we obtain the assurance for that day through this love, and all the while fulfilling this most basic command of our Lord."[21]

Chapter five of this letter summarized the thoughts of John. In dealing with a heresy such as Gnosticism, John described the struggles of the Christian and the faith of the Christian and compared these tenets with the weakness of this heresy. John reaffirmed that the Christian must love the brethren. This love was not practiced by Gnostics who often ridiculed the spiritual inferiority of their brethren. John reinforced the concept that the Christian had to keep the commands of God. The Gnostics believed that behavior did not matter, and that the Christian could act in any way. John insisted that conduct did matter and was basic to a proper belief in God. Wuest wrote that the Christian had to recognize that he was in a struggle with the forces of evil. The Christian was surrounded by these forces and must depend on God to win this incessant battle.[22]

Finally, the Christian must absolutely demonstrate faith in Jesus as the Son of God. "Who is he who is constantly coming off victorious over the world but the one who believes that Jesus is the Son of God" (1 John 5:5). This kind of faith was unknown to Cerinthus and other Gnostics. Wuest commented, "The combination Jesus Christ used together by John to designate one individual, is a refutation of the Cerinthian Gnostic heresy to the effect that Jesus was the person, only human, not deity, and that the Christ or divine element came upon Him at His baptism and left Him before His death on the Cross."[23]

This fifth chapter of John's first letter has always been a chapter of great confidence. John was emphatic that we know that we have eternal life. Lenski commented that John assured in order to combat the heresies of the Gnostics who denounced the way of the Christ: "The readers must know this with a clear mental perception in order to meet and to refute these Gnostic heretics when they come with the claim that they are the ones who know."[24] John also told his readers "that if we ask anything according to His will, He hears us" (1 John 5:14).

In the closing verses of this chapter, John mentioned a sin unto death. If we remember his earlier statements about sin, we are reminded of committing an individual sin in contrast to continuing in a constant state of sin. John was not counting individual sins as sins unto death, but rather a life dedicated to sin. He stated, "We know that anyone born of God does not continue to sin" (1 John 5:18). John recognized that the Son of God came and gave the believer true understanding that culminates in eternal life (John 5:20). Ross observed this was the consuming thought of John's life at this point; it was the expression that John had to write once more "before he lays down his pen."[25] Stott added, "It undermines the whole structure of the heretics' theology. It concerned the Son of God, through whom alone we can be rescued from the evil one and delivered from the world."[26]

With these closing thoughts, John presented a warning that at first seems unusual. Yet the warning was certain in the context of the entire letter. As Lenski made clear, the idols about whom John warned were all the anti-trinitarian conceptions of God, no matter by whom they were held.[27] Throughout this letter John elevated Jesus Christ as the Son of God, the one who came in the flesh to love us and to promise us eternal life. Our conduct must reflect the love of Christ in our attitudes toward others. Hatred, contempt, and discord must be banished from the Christian's life. If we continue in love, the assurance of an eternity with God will await us.

JOHN'S SECOND LETTER

The writer identified himself as the elder in this brief letter. John referred to his reader as an elect lady. Commentators such as Wuest believed the lady to be a homeowner in the area of Ephesus where "her home was the meeting place of the local assembly."[1] *The Expositor's Greek Testament* observed that it was not uncommon for a wealthy member of the assembly (such as Philemon to whom Paul wrote) to host the assembly in his own home.[2] Whether John was referring to an actual person or simply referring to the congregation as the elect lady is certainly not the most important issue of the letter.

This letter again contrasted truth and love with heresy and falsehood. This particular congregation must have been experiencing the heresies of the Ephesian region. John identified love as the mark of the Christian church. Lenski commented, "This is the spiritual love which in First John is made one of the outstanding marks of all true Christians. The antichristian heretics and deceivers have no love for the members of the true church; they try to tear it to pieces."[3]

Great joy

The text of the letter expressed John's great joy that some of his children were walking in the truth. There was adequate inference in this statement that John realized that there were some who were not walking in the truth. The love that John again talked about in this letter was in synchronization with God's commandments. John was still dealing with heresies from the first letter. Now an entire congregation had to make a decision; this congregation was besieged by those who denied Christ. As Wuest put it, "The person, therefore, who goes beyond the teaching of the incarnation of the Son in human flesh, thus denying the incarnation, does not possess God in a saving relationship."[4]

In many ways the second letter was also a precursor to the third letter attributed to John. John was identifying those who resisted the truth such as the leader Diotrophes. Lenski muses, "How all this applies to Diotrophes and to his clique is plain. He hated John himself although John was an apostle; he closed the door of hospitality to John's missionaries, threatened the members who would receive them, and opened the door to Gnostic proselytes." Later Lenski surmised, "John does not name Diotrophes in this letter to the congregation. John is not settling with the opposition by means of this letter; he is coming in person to do that."[5]

Doctrine in love

In the second letter John stressed pure doctrine in Christ over the heresies of the proud unbelievers, those who had denied Jesus Christ as Lord. John could not tolerate this unbelief, the very essence of anti-Christian behavior. He made it clear that he would uphold doctrine as well as agape love. The two did not exclude one another.

JOHN'S THIRD LETTER

The third letter attributed to John was well-crafted with plots and subplots. The letter was a microcosm of the first-century church with parallels through the years even to the present. The letter identified three members of a congregation: Gaius, Diotrophes, and Demetrius.

The first mentioned was Gaius, clearly a favorite of John. Gaius was a popular name in the Roman world, even used by the Caesars. This Gaius has sometimes been spoken of as the Gaius of Derbe (Acts 20:4). Although this cannot be completely verified, John commended this Gaius for his spiritual health and hoped that his physical health would improve and prosper as had his spiritual health. Stott observed that the prosperity gospel message, so popular through the years, was quickly disproved as this man had experienced physical difficulties while excelling in spiritual wealth.[1] Ross further commented that, even today, many are concerned about the health of their bodies, "but they never give a thought to their souls."[2]

Gaius was an extraordinary everyday Christian. He represented everyman as a Christian. John considered Gaius to be one of the faithful spiritual children and used the term *beloved* to express his appreciation of Gaius' life. Roberts suggested that Gaius was a convert of John: "A preacher delights to know that those whom he has converted and has helped to mature in Christ are being faithful to what has been taught." The chief contribution of Gaius was the physical and spiritual support he rendered to his brethren. "Gaius was being loyal to the responsibilities of Christian love and to the truth which he had espoused, perhaps also to the reputation which he had earned among the brethren."[3]

A more striking contrast could not be shown than the daunting figure of Diotrophes found in the ninth verse. Gaius had pure, loving, and altruistic motives while Diotrophes reflected the arrogant and domineering attitudes of the Gnostics. John described him as one who had to have his way. Ross thought he had "utter contempt of the teachings of Jesus."[4] John's mission clearly was to confront this rebellious, pompous villain when he visited the area. Diotrophes was the leading heretic of the area and likely was one of the Gnostics who despised the truth and the true believers such as Gaius. A power struggle was taking place, and John was willing to enter the fray, knowing that truth guided by love would win.

The letter concluded with the commendation of Demetrius, a little known Christian of this congregation. Demetrius was probably better known to John as one of the faithful preachers and as a preacher who would receive the assistance of Gaius. Roberts conjectured that "the natural inference is that he was one of the traveling preachers of the gospel whom the elder had mentioned to Gaius and encouraged him to entertain. Quite likely he was the bearer of this letter to Gaius."[5] Who would win the battle for truth in this congregation? There was no doubt. John and the forces of truth would triumph over the forces of an arrogant heresy. Lenski was right when he stated that John would settle the Gnostic problem in this church personally, for John was never afraid to defend the truth. "As the apostle Paul, he was not ashamed of the gospel for it is the power of salvation not only to the Jew but to the Gentile as well."[6]

SUMMARY OF THE LETTERS

In summary, conservative scholars have overwhelmingly attributed the authorship of these three letters to John. David Smith in *The Expositor's Greek Testament* especially noted the similarities between John's gospel and his first letter: "It is beyond reasonable doubt that the Epistle and the Gospel are from the same pen. They agree in style, language, and thought." The second and third letters usually focused on John's self-description as the elder (*presbuteros*) and to its meaning. Smith again wrote, "There is no doubt that the Second and Third Epistles are from the same hand." And in reference to the use of the word *elder* in the salutation, he added, "The second generation of Christians used it of their predecessors, the men of early days."[1] John was one of the last survivors of the early days and confidently described himself as the elder one.

Wayne Meeks wrote about urban Christians of the first century. He concluded, "Not only was there a mixture of social levels in each congregation; but also in each individual or category that we are able to identify there is evidence of divergent rankings in the different dimensions of status."[2] The letters of John addressed all of these levels, and his teachings have applied to each level. The letters can be summarized in these conclusive findings of truth:

1. The greatest doctrine for John was the divine and human nature of Jesus Christ. Throughout his letters John saw Jesus as the divine revelation of God. Jesus was from the eternal, yet seen with human eyes and touched with human hands. He stated that Jesus was the light and without sin in contrast to the sinful nature of mankind who lived in darkness. Jesus obliterated the power of sin by the shedding of His blood, and this blood continuously cleansed the believer of the power of sin.

2. John taught that this world will end, but those who walk in the light of Jesus Christ will live forever. Jesus promised eternal life although the glory of our eternal bodies has not yet been revealed. This process of eternal life has begun even while the Christian is living in this world.

3. John taught us *agape* love. This love was divine in nature, coming from God. *Agape* love was love for the brethren, and indeed for all of humanity. This love was inclusive, not exclusive, and proved itself in action and not in word. This love increased the boldness of the Christian in all things righteous, and this love alleviated a sense of doubt or fear in regard to salvation.

4. The greatest sin was the denial of Jesus Christ as the Son of God. This anti-Christian spirit enveloped some of the so-called believers in these letters. This sin was secured by a false arrogant knowledge that elevated self and denied the power of Christ. The one who denied Christ also denied spiritual life to himself.

LIFE IN THE LATER YEARS

As this book has been primarily a history of John, the Apostle, it would be good to review his personal journey so far. The biography has of necessity included his writings for these writings also reflect his character. John began his ministry for Christ as a young fisherman. He had been educated well for a middle class son of a tradesman. He was capable of writing and speaking his own language of Aramaic as well as Greek, the language of commerce and diplomacy. In this respect he was above average as most of his countrymen were not able to read or write. His family was bourgeois in almost every sense and was probably part of a fishing consortium that included Simon Peter's family. With his brother James and his mother and father very closely involved, we have the picture of a provincial and yet progressive family. In all likelihood, John in later years received some investment income from the family business that he probably sold after the deaths of his brother and father.

From all indications, he had no history of marriage, although one can never be certain in these matters for the scriptures revealed Peter's marriage only through his mother-in-law's illness and the comments of the Apostle Paul. The patristic writings traditionally regarded John as a celibate throughout life, and the scriptures never mention that he was married. From every indication, the apostles who remained unmarried did so by choice and not by command. Constant danger and uncertainty of the future often dictated that the single life was the better one for the apostles.

Role of leadership

We have noticed that he was in the inner three circle of Jesus, though at first he was third on the list. Peter also assumed leadership, and James always preceded his brother in the synoptic gospel narratives. At first John revealed a vindictive, volatile personality. He was very exclusive in nature and limited in vision. There were indications that his family knew the religious leaders as he was able to enter the inner court at the trial of Jesus. We have noticed that John's gospel was different from the other gospels. Smalley, in his book *John Evangelist and Interpreter*, wrote that "John did not rewrite the Synoptics but was rather preserving in his own way a Christian tradition parallel to theirs."[1] We also have seen that his gospel portrayed a different picture of him, especially in the last years of the ministry of Jesus. He alone was at the cross; he alone was given the care of Mary; he described himself as the disciple of special relationship with Jesus. He had radically changed his life from his early years.

We can conclude that in his later years John desired to write a gospel. Smalley conjectured AD 80 as a possible date, after John moved to Ephesus, though possibly by AD 70. This gospel was different in many respects from the other three, but as Smalley indicated, "It was grounded in historical tradition when it departs from the Synoptics, as well as when it overlaps with them."[2] The gospel was a summation, a personal memoir, and an ode of love to his Christ. R.H. Lightfoot stated that the gospel was in perfect balance with Jesus as God and man; also, it was unique in that this gospel began in heaven and closed on earth.[3]

By this time John had certainly been honored as one of the last links to Jesus. Certainly he would have had encouragement from the churches in the area of Ephesus to write such a gospel. At this time John assumed the role of the elder one, the honored one, a title of great respect. He became a fatherly figure who visited the churches surrounding Ephesus. These places in Asia Minor were well-known to John. As Paul did years before, John visited cities of the region and knew the individual congregations and loved each one dearly.

Somewhere in the years AD 80–90 John became part of a larger assignment. Meeks commented that individual households in various cities recognized "being part of a larger movement." Meeks added, "No group can persist for any appreciable time without some patterns of leadership, some differentiation of roles among its members, some means of managing conflict, some ways of articulating shared values and norms, and some sanctions to assure acceptable levels of conformity to those norms."[4] In this situation, John became the paternal mentor. He, as Paul with the Corinthians and Galatians, confronted the internal and external problems of each congregation. John's robust energy belied his advanced age, and he became the de facto guardian of the churches of Asia Minor. He never retired from service to Christ, and he willingly assumed this mantle of leadership in Ephesus. He continued to amaze with his writings, his love for the brethren, and his zeal in dealing with the enemies of the brotherhood. As an old man John thrived in a great metropolis, never retreating to a pleasant place of seclusion. Surely his work for the Lord was coming to an end. Yet there was more.

THE VISIONS

"And I saw a new heaven and a new earth: for the first heaven and the first earth were passed away; and there was no more sea. And I John saw the holy city, new Jerusalem, coming down from God out of heaven, prepared as a bride adorned for her husband. And I heard a great voice out of heaven saying, 'Behold the tabernacle of God is with men, and He will dwell with them, and they shall be His people, and God himself shall be with them, and be their God. And God shall wipe away all tears from their eyes; and there shall be no more death, neither sorrow, nor crying, neither shall there be any more pain: for the former things are passed away.'"(Revelation 21:1–4)

Persecution under Domitian

When John wrote these words through the Holy Spirit, his secure world at Ephesus had radically changed. In the year AD 81 Domitian had become emperor. Michael Grant described his reign as "a meticulously thought-out policy of destruction."[1] John was both to prosper and suffer during this emperor's rule which ended with Domitian's assassination in 96. Grant observed that this emperor's last three years were full of paranoia. In Grant's extensive study of the Roman emperors, he wrote about Domitian's intensified policy to track down Jews. Furthermore, he collected an odious tax called the *fiscus Judaicus* and condemned any people who adopted Jewish customs describing such customs as atheism since these ways avoided any sacrifice to the emperor. In his book, *The World of Rome*, Grant recognized the change that Christianity had made, especially in the lower classes. He credited John with incorporating Greek philosophical terms in the gospel message, and the message with offering hope, something Epicureans denied. This hope alleviated the suffering that the "Stoics grimly accepted."[2]

The divinity of the emperor was an idea that had germinated from the days of Augustus.[3] John had been aware of this divine claim even when living in Judea. Yet, as the Apostle Paul had done, John attempted to live under the authorities as much as possible. He had to deal with the vacillations of the individual emperors. For the most part, Augustus and Tiberius caused no major problems to Jews or Christians, but Nero had found the Christians an easy target, especially in Rome. Aquila and Priscilla felt the temporary wrath of Claudius. Still, Paul did not lash out against Rome which had offered him a sense of protection. John also did not seem to have any clash with the Romans during the writing of the gospel and the letters.

When we come to the last book attributed to John—Revelation or the Apocalypse—the enemy was clearly Rome. Christians were being assaulted with an intense persecution by the government. After years of dealing with internal problems of the church at Ephesus and surrounding cities, John was confronted in AD 95 with life-threatening situations. At the time of the writing of Revelation, John was in exile on the small Greek island in the Mediterranean called Patmos. Robert Wilken observed in his book *The Christians as the Romans Saw Them* that Domitian had "exiled distinguished citizens, accused some of his own provincial governors of conspiracy, and driven from public life good and able men. In this atmosphere of fear and suspicion good men were unwilling to speak their minds to friends lest they be implicated as traitors and summarily whisked off to exile or death."[4]

John, the right person for the apocalyptic writings

The Revelation itself has been attributed by most conservative scholars to John the Apostle. Lenski wrote, "Until the time of Origen and including him the whole church knew of only one John i.e., the apostle." Lenski observed that the book contained the special wording of apocalyptic writing. "The Lord intended the language of Revelation to be different from that of John's other writings."[5] Leon Morris agreed that this John was the author saying, "Only one John was great enough among the Christians to need no description."[6] The question has always been present as to why John was chosen to be the writer. The other gospel writers could not have predicted such a choice. These writers at times focused on John's poor attitudes and the attitudes of his family. They did mention him as a member of the circle whom Christ took into His confidence, but they did not describe John in visionary or compassionate terms. As has already been discussed, Luke in Acts, chapter fifteen, acknowledged that John had grown to be one of the pillars of the church. The time of this fifteenth chapter was about AD 50. Yet, most of John's spiritual progress was documented in his own writings.

At the age of at least 90, John seemed an unlikely writer for the most mystical book in the New Testament. But all of John's life had prepared him. As a Jew, he would be familiar with the apocalyptic writings of the Old Testament. He had no doubt studied the writings of Daniel and Ezekiel. John was open to the mysteries of God as no other New Testament writer, except perhaps Paul. And God had a plan for John even beyond the plans for the Apostle Paul. John was to receive the visions of what was to come for Christians. These visions aptly called the Apocalypse or Revelation have been the subject of endless comments, speculations, and volumes.

John's authorship of Revelation

Conservative scholar William Hendriksen wrote one of the best commentaries on Revelation, *More Than Conquerors*. Hendriksen expressed the strong conviction that John the Apostle was the author, guided directly by the Holy Spirit. Hendriksen cited the traditions of the church of the first two centuries including such notables as Justin Martyr, Irenaeus, Clement of Alexandria, Tertullian, and Origen, all of whom ascribed the book to John the Apostle. Hendriksen also believed the date of authorship as AD 95–96 as opposed to earlier dates. "When we add to all this that according to a very strong tradition the apostle John was banished to the isle of Patmos, and that he spent the closing years of his life at Ephesus, to which the first of the seven epistles of the Apocalypse was addressed, the conclusion that the last book of the Bible was written by the disciple whom Jesus loved is inescapable."[7]

J. W. Roberts also agreed that this book was written by John the Apostle in his later years. He described the conditions of the church at Ephesus and surrounding cities as much different from the time of Paul in the decades of the 50s and 60s. The conditions were different from the times when Peter wrote to the Christians who had just settled in Asia Minor. There were new opponents, new compromises, and new hazards including severe persecutions. There were references to indifference in some churches and to great wealth in others. Roberts also selected a later date, in the 90s, since Laodicea had materially recovered from an earthquake that Tacitus had recorded there in AD 60.[8] Roberts espoused the view that John was especially concerned with the churches in his venue. Persecutions were eminent and warnings must be issued. The emperor

Domitian was to be feared. "As the decades passed, the dark cloud on the horizon was the rise and spread of the cult of emperor worship."[9]

With these observations in mind, the first three chapters of Revelation are essential in identifying the author. Since the work is one filled with visions and symbols, what John saw at the beginning of his work and then transmitted to his readers is most important.

John's relationship to the churches of Asia Minor

He spoke of himself in the first chapter as the servant of Jesus Christ and the brother to the seven churches that are in Asia Minor. At this time no other writer was eligible for this claim. Peter and Paul had been martyred, according to every tradition. Only John had labored extensively with the seven churches, and only John had made his residence in Ephesus for over twenty years.

John set the tone of the letter in the first chapter when he declared his own sharing of tribulation with the seven churches. This number seven was the number of completion and perfection in Jewish writings.[10] It became the first prominent symbol of the book with many more to follow. What John saw in visionary form and was told to write became the most brilliant apocalypse in scripture. He was directed to write, and the words he wrote were words of prophesy. God as the Alpha and Omega gave John the authority to write. Only the Apostle John of Ephesus, who knew the seven churches intimately, could be entrusted with giving these congregations the good and bad news. Concurring with William Ramsay and other scholars, Roberts described the prophecies as reflecting an intimate knowledge of these fellowships including the "history, topography, economics, and religious life of the cities where the churches were located."[11]

The problems of these seven churches varied. John addressed the individual needs of each one. He wrote words of praise, encouragement, warning, and condemnation. The church at Laodicea has historically borne the brunt of criticism from ministers because of its wealth and inertia. Ironically, this was the city that had raced to rebuild itself after that terrible earthquake of AD 60. But there were commendable churches such as Philadelphia and Smyrna. Most congregations were in the average range such as Ephesus, whose priorities were not as focused on Christ as in earlier times. The letters to the churches warned of impending dangers. Gone were the days of Roman protection that saved evangelists such as Paul at Corinth. In his book, *Ancient Corinth*, Nicos Papahatzis reminded us that the success of Paul's ventures in that Greek city were largely because of the magistrate Gallio's decision "that Paul's teachings did not constitute an offense under Roman Law."[12] Rather, John had to prepare his people for persecution, even death, at the hands of authorities.

The ultimate message of the Revelation

The fear of death and the afterlife was of great concern to the classical world. In his book *The Greeks*, Kenneth Dover reviewed the predominant philosophies of the time. The Stoics had found the soul to be some part of a greater universe, and for the Epicureans "removal of the fear of divine punishment was crucial."[13] For most of the ancient world, death was a great mystery and future existence uncertain. Robert Garland wrote about the predominant view of death in the Greek mind as one where "the dead as perceived by the living were in a very literal sense mere shadows of their former selves."[14] John prepared his readers for the uncertainty of life after death. How much of John's visions were intended for the people of his day, the so-called preterist view, and how much was intended for future generations, deemed the futurist view, has never been solved, and will always be discussed. There can be no doubt that symbols such as Babylon referred to the dangers of Rome. The numerology of seven, twenty-four, and 144,000 would have been familiar to those Christians of that day who had some background in apocalyptic literature.

John saw glimpses of heaven that only Paul and Stephen had viewed. Unlike them, he gave us a much more detailed panorama of the future life. He promised his readers a final victory and a return of their Lord in triumph. John's heavenly visions included the martyrs and their white robes. He saw a new world with people from every nation, every race, and too numerous to count. He saw a city, the new Jerusalem, adorned as a bride for her husband.

The ancient cities were much like the cities of the modern world, full of greed and danger. The Roman writer Juvenal satirized his city of Rome: "But here in Rome we must toe the line of fashion, living beyond our means, and often on borrowed credit."[15] Juvenal wrote of buildings collapsing, constant noise at night and endless traffic and chaos. But John saw an idealized city where tears were wiped away and the old dangers of earthly life had passed away. The symbols of this city were described as gorgeous: streets of gold, jeweled buildings, everlasting day with none of the fears of the night. The book, *Heaven, a History*, described both Paul and John's concept of the heavenly city. For Paul another house has been prepared that housed the soul's heavenly body. This move from earth to heaven necessitated the death of the old body. For John, as well as Jesus and Paul, this heaven was God-centered. In Revelation, no natural elements such as the sun and moon were needed because of the bright light of God's eternal presence. *Heaven, a History* pictured the new Jerusalem as "designed for the blessed; imitating a temple, it served as the final place for their full and total communion with God."[16]

What was the final message of this most intriguing of apocalyptic writings? Hendricksen believed it to be ultimate victory for the Christian. "Not the Devil but Christ is victorious. God's plan though for a while seemingly—never really—defeated, in the end is seen to triumph completely. Conquerors are we. Nay, more than conquerors, for not only are we delivered from the greatest curse, yea, from every curse, but we obtain the most glorious blessing besides, Rev.21:3."[17] This message gave hope to the persecuted churches of John's time and would give hope to all Christians in future times battling the forces of evil.

AFTER THE VISIONS

After the writing of Revelation and the death of Domitian, John returned to Ephesus. Myths abounded about his seeming immortality, including the story that he continued to live even while entombed. Godet reached the safest conclusion that John died a few years after his return from exile. He commented, "There is nothing improbable in this." Consequently, John might have been in personal relationship with many younger Christians such as Polycarp who would have seen John and known his teachings.[1] He never became reclusive. He was the beloved disciple, the blessed believer, the spiritual father. His final message was one of love toward God and toward the entire world. Yet, John was always that fiery defender of Jesus Christ and the truth of Jesus' teachings. John has been underestimated for years and neglected for centuries. Living a long life full of wonder and mystery, John was privileged to see what no other mortal had seen, and ultimately, he has blessed all generations by his life and writings.

SELECTED SOURCES

Armstrong, Karen. *Holy War*. New York: Anchor Books, 2001.

Armstrong, W. P. "Chronicles of the New Testament." *The International Bible Encyclopedia*. Grand Rapids, Michigan: Wm. B. Eerdmans, 1960.

Avidad, Nahman. *Discovering Jerusalem*. Nashville: Thomas Nelson Publishers, 1983.

Bernard, J. H. *A Critical and Exegetical Commentary on the Gospel According to St. John*. Edinburgh: T. and T. Clark, Ltd., 1976.

Birley, Anthony. *Lives of the Later Caesars*. London: Penguin Books, 1976.

Bourbon, F. *Lost Civilizations*. New York: Barnes and Noble, 1999.

Braaten, Carl and Robert Jensen. *The Last Things*. Grand Rapids, Michigan: Wm. B. Eerdmans, 2002.

Bruce, F.F. *The Acts of the Apostles*. London: Tyndale Press, 1956.

Bruce, F.F. *New Testament History*. Garden City, New York: Doubleday, 1980.

Burns, A.R. *The Penguin History of Greece*. London: Penguin Books, 1985.

Butler, Paul T. *What the Bible Says About Civil Government*. Joplin, Missouri: College Press, 1990.

Copleston, Frederick. *A History of Philosophy.* Vol. 1. Garden City, New York: Image Books, 1962.

Dana, H.E. *The New Testament World.* Nashville: Broadman Press, 1937.

Dods, Marcus. *The Expositors Greek Testament.* Grand Rapids, Michigan: Wm. B. Eerdmans, 1956.

Dover, Kenneth. *The Greeks.* Austin, Texas: The University of Texas Press, 1986.

Eusebius. *The Ecclesiastical History.* Grand Rapids, Michigan: Baker Book House, 1991.

Garland, Robert. *The Greek Way of Death.* Ithaca, New York: Cornell University Press, 1985.

Godet, Frederick. *Commentary on the Gospel of John.* Grand Rapids, Michigan: Zondervan, 1886.

Gower, Ralph. *The New Manners and Customs of Bible Times.* Chicago: Moody Press, 1987.

Grant, Michael. *The Twelve Caesars.* New York: Barnes and Noble, 1996.

Grant, Michael. *The World of Rome.* New York: Mentor Books, 1960.

Green, Peter. *Alexander of Macedon 356-323 B.C.* Berkeley: University of California Press, 1991.

Green, Peter. *Ancient Greece.* New York: Thames and Hudson, 1987.

Henriksen, William. *More Than Conquerors.* Grand Rapids, Michigan: Baker Book House, 1970.

Juvenal, *Juvenal. The Sixteen Satires.* London: Penguin Books, 1974.

Lenski, R.C.H. *The Interpretation of I and II Epistles of Peter, The Three Epistles of John, and The Epistle of Jude.* Minneapolis: Augsburg Publishing House, 1969.

Lenski, R.C.H. *The Interpretation of St. John's Revelation.* Minneapolis: Augsburg Publishing House, 1961.

Levick, Barbara. *Tiberius the Politician*. London and New York: Routledge, 1999.

Lightfoot, R.H. *St. John's Gospel*. Oxford: Oxford University Press, 1972.

McDannell, Colleen and Bernhard Lang. *Heaven a History*. New Haven: Yale University Press, 1988.

Meeks, Wayne A. *The First Urban Christians*. New Haven: Yale University Press.

Moo, Douglas. *The Letter of James*. Grand Rapids, Michigan: Wm. B. Eerdmans, 1999.

Morris, Leon. *The Book of Revelation*. Grand Rapids, Michigan: Wm.B. Eerdmans, 1999.

Murphy-O'Connor, Jerome. *The Holy Land*. Oxford: Oxford University Press, 1986.

Nappo, Salvatore. *Pompeii*, a *Guide to the Ancient City*. New York: Barnes and Noble, 1998.

Orr, James. "Jesus Christ." *The International Standard Bible Encyclopedia*. Grand Rapids, Michigan: Wm. B. Eerdmans, 1960.

Pack, Frank. *The Gospel According to John*. Austin, Texas: Sweet Publishing Company, 1975.

Papahatzis, Nicos. *Ancient Corinth*. Athens: Ekdotike Athenon, 2001.

Patrick, G.T.W. *Heraclitus of Ephesus*. Chicago: Argonaut Inc., 1969.

Plummer, Alfred. *A Critical and Exegetical Commentary on the Gospel According to S. Luke*. Edinburgh: T and T Clark, 1960.

Rackl, Hans-Wolf. *Discovering the Past Archeology under Water*. New York: Charles Scribner, 1968.

Ramsay, William. *St. Paul The Traveler and Roman Citizen*, Grand Rapids, Michigan: Kregel Publications, 2001.

Reinhold, Meyer. *Hellas and Rome*. New York: New American Library, 1972.

Roberts, J.W. *The Letter of James*. Austin, Texas: Sweet Publishing Company, 1977.

Roberts, J.W. *The Letters of John*. Austin, Texas: Sweet Publishing Company, 1968.

Roberts, J. W. *The Revelation to John*. Austin, Texas: Sweet Publishing Company, 1974.

Ross, Alexander. *The Epistles of James and John*. Grand Rapids, Michigan: Wm. B. Eerdmans, 1974.

Runciman, Steven. *The History of the Crusades*. Cambridge: Cambridge University Press, 1968.

Seutonius. *The Lives of the Twelve Caesars*. New York: Random House, 1959.

Shanks, Hershel. A series of articles about James, the brother of Jesus, and the ossuary findings. *Biblical Archaeology Review*. Washington, 2003.

Smalley, Stephen S. *John, Evangelist and Interpreter*. Downers Grove, Illinois: Intervarsity Press, 1998.

Smith, David. *The Expositors Greek Testament*. Grand Rapids, Michigan: Wm. B. Eerdmans, 1956.

Southern, Pat. *Augustus*. London and New York: Routledge, 1999.

Speller, Elizabeth. *Following Hadrian*. Oxford: Oxford University Press, 2003.

Stott, J.R.W. *The Letters of John*. Grand Rapids, Michigan: Wm. B. Eerdmans, 1996.

Taylor, Lily Ross. *The Divinity of the Roman Emperor*. Middletown, Connecticut: Scholars Press, 1931.

Tacitus. *The Annals of Imperial Rome*. London: Penguin Books, 1996.

Thucydides. *The Landmark Thucydides*. New York: The Free Press, 1996.

Warner, Rex. *The Greek Philosophers*. New York: The New American Library, 1958.

Westcott, B.F. *The Gospel According to St. John.* Grand Rapids, Michigan: Wm. B. Eerdmans, 1958.

Wilken, Robert. *The Christians As the Romans Saw Them.* New Haven: Yale University Press, 2003.

Wuest, Kenneth S. *In These Last Days.* Grand Rapids, Michigan: Wm. B. Eerdmans, 1957.

END NOTES

Introduction

1. *The New Testament World*, H. E. Dana, 1937, Broadman Press, Nashville

Chapter One, The Son of Zebedee

1. *The Twelve Caesars*, Michael Grant, 1996, Barnes and Noble, New York

2. *The Lives of the Twelve Caesars*, Seutonius, 1959, Random House, New York

3. *Augustus*, Pat Southern, 1999, Routledge, London and New York

4. *The International Bible Encyclopedia*, W.P. Armstrong, 1960, "Chronology of the New Testament," Wm. B. Eerdmans, Grand Rapids, Michigan

5. *The New Testament World*, H.E. Dana

6. *What the Bible Says about Civil Government*, Paul T. Butler, 1990, College Press, Joplin, Missouri

7. *New Testament History*, F.F. Bruce, 1980, Doubleday, Garden City, New York

8. *Ibid*

9.   *The Annals of Imperial Rome*, Tacitus, 1996, Penguin Books, London

10.   *The Twelve Caesars*, Michael Grant

11.   *Tiberius, The Politician*, Barbara Levick, 1999, Routledge, London and New York

12.   *New Testament History*, F.F. Bruce

13.   *The New Testament World*, H.E. Dana

Chapter Two, James and John

1.   *A Critical and Exegetical Commentary on the Gospel According to S. Luke*, Alfred Plummer, 1960, The International Critical Commentary, T and T Clark, Edinburgh

Chapter Three, John According to John

1.   *The Gospel According to St. John*, B.F. Westcott, 1958, Wm.B. Eerdmans, Grand Rapids, Michigan

2.   *Commentary on the Gospel of John*, Frederick L. Godet, 1886, Zondervan, Grand Rapids, Michigan

3.   *The Expositor's Greek Testament*, Marcus Dods, 1956, Wm.B. Eerdmans, Grand Rapids, Michigan

4.   *Ibid*

Chapter Four, John in Jerusalem

1.   *The Gospel According to St. John*, B.F. Westcott

2.   *New Testament History*, F.F. Bruce

3.   *The Annals of Rome*, Tacitus

4.   *Juvenal, The Sixteen Satires*, Juvenal, 1974, Penguin Books, London

5.   *The Lives of the Twelve Caesars*, Seutonius

6. *The Twelve Caesars*, Michael Grant
7. *New Testament History*, F.F. Bruce

Chapter Five, Acts and Beyond

1. *The Acts of the Apostles*, F.F. Bruce, 1956, Tyndale Press, London
2. *Ibid*
3. *Ibid*
4. A Series of articles about James, the brother of Jesus and the ossuary findings, Hershel Shanks, 2003, *Biblical Archaeology Review*, Washington
5. *The Twelve Caesars*, Michael Grant
6. *The Lives of the Twelve Caesars*, Seutonius
7. *The Twelve Caesars*, Michael Grant
8. *Ibid*
9. *Holy War*, Karen Armstrong, 2001, Anchor Books, New York
10. *Ibid*
11. *The Ecclesiastical History*, Eusebius,1991, Baker Book House, Grand Rapids, Michigan

Chapter Six, John in Ephesus

1. *The Letter of James*, Douglas Moo, 1999, Wm.B. Eerdmans, Grand Rapids, Michigan
2. *The First Urban Christians*, Wayne A. Meeks, 2003, Yale University Press, New Haven and London
3. *Heraclitus of Ephesus*, G.T.W. Patrick, 1969, Argonaut Inc. Publishers, Chicago
4. *The Greek Philosophers*, Rex Warner, 1958, The New American Library, New York
5. *A History of Philosophy*, Vol. I, Frederick Copleston, 1962, Image Books, Garden City, New York

6. *Lost Civilizations*, F. Bourbon, Editor, 1999, Barnes and Noble, New York

7. *Hellas and Rome*, Meyer Reinhold, 1972, New American Library, New York

8. *Ancient Greece*, Peter Green, 1987, Thames and London, New York

9. *The Landmark Thucydides*, Thucydides, 1996, The Free Press, New York

10. *The World of Rome*, Michael Grant, 1960, Mentor Books, The New American Library, New York

11. *Alexander of Macedon, 356-323 B.C.*, Peter Green, 1991, The University of California Press, Berkeley

12. *The Annals of Imperial Rome*, Tacitus

13. *The Penguin History of Greece*, A.R. Burns, 1985, Penguin Books, London

14. *The Acts of the Apostles,* F. F. Bruce

15. *Ibid*

16. *The Gospel According to St. John*, B.F.Westcott

17. *Ibid*

18. *Commentary on the Gospel of John*, Frederick L. Godet

19. *Ibid*

20. *The Ecclesiastical History*, Eusebius

21. *Ibid*

22. *Ibid*

23. *St, Paul The Traveler and Roman Citizen*, William Ramsay, 2001, Kregel Publications, Grand Rapids, Michigan

24. *Lives of the Later Caesars*, Anthony Birley, 1976, Penguin Books, London

25. *Following Hadrian*, Elizabeth Speller, 2003, Oxford University Press, Oxford

Chapter Seven, The Gospel

1. *The Letter of James,* J.W. Roberts, 1977, Sweet Publishing Company, Austin, Texas

2. *The Gospel According to John*, Frank Pack, 1975, Sweet Publishing Company, Austin, Texas

3. *The Gospel According to St. John*, B.F. Westcott

4. *The Gospel According to John*, Frank Pack

5. *Commentary on the Gospel of John*, Frederick L. Godet

6. *The Gospel According to St. John*, B. F. Westcott

7. *Commentary on the Gospel of John*, Frederick L. Godet

8. *Pompeii, A Guide to the Ancient City*, Salvatore Nappo, 1998, Barnes and Noble, New York

9. *The First Urban Christians*, Wayne Meeks

10. *The Holy Land*, Jerome Murphy-O'Connor, 1986, Oxford University Press, Oxford

11. *The History of the Crusades*, Steven Runciman, 1968, Cambridge at the University Press, Cambridge

12. *The Gospel According to John*, Frank Pack

13. *Ibid*

14. *The Expositor's Greek Testament*, Marcus Dods

15. *The Gospel According to John*, Frank Pack

16. *Ibid*

17. *The Gospel According to St. John*, B.F. Westcott

18. *Ibid*

19. *The Gospel According to John*, Frank Pack

20. *The Gospel According to St. John*, B.F. Westcott

21. *Ibid*

22. *The Gospel According to John*, Frank Pack

23. *The Gospel According to St. John*, B.F. Westcott

24. *The International Standard Bible Encyclopedia,* "Jesus Christ," James Orr

25. *The Gospel According to St. John*, B.F. Westcott

26. *A Critical and Exegetical Commentary on the Gospel According to St. John*, J. H. Bernard, 1976, T and T Clark, Edinburgh

27. *The Gospel According to John*, Frank Pack

28. *Commentary on the Gospel of John*, Frederick L. Godet

29. *The Gospel According to John*, Frank Pack

30. *A Critical and Exegetical Commentary on the Gospel According to St. John*, J. J. Bernard

31. *The Gospel According to St. John*, B.F. Westcott

32. *The New Manners and Customs of Bible Times*, Ralph Gower, 1987, Moody Press, Chicago

33. *The Expositors Greek Testament*, Marcus Dods

34. *Ibid*

35. *The Gospel According to St. John*, B.F. Westcott

36. *Ibid*

Chapter Eight, John's First Letter

1. *Discovering Jerusalem*, Nahman Avigad, 1983, Thomas Nelson Publishers, Nashville

2. *Discovering the Past Archaeology Under Water*, Hans-Wolf Rackl, 1968, Charles Scribner, New York

3. *The Letters of John*, J.R.W. Stott, 1996, Wm.B. Eerdmans, Grand Rapids, Michigan

4. *The Interpretation of I and II Epistles of Peter, The Three Epistles of John, and The Epistle of Jude*, R.C.H. Lenski, 1969, Augsburg Publishing House, Minneapolis

5. *The Letters of John*, J.R.W. Stott

6.   *Ibid*

7.   *In These Last Days*, Kenneth S. Wuest, 1957, Wm.B.Eerdmans, Grand Rapids, Michigan

8.   *The Interpretation of I and II Epistles of Peter, The Three Epistles of John, and The Epistle of Jude*, R.C.H. Lenski

9.   *The Epistles of James and John*, Alexander Ross, 1974, Wm. B. Eerdmans, Grand Rapids, Michigan

10. *In These Last Days*, Kenneth S. Wuest

11. *The Letters of John*, J.R.W. Stott

12. *The Epistles of James and John*, Alexander Ross

13. *In These Last Days*, Kenneth S. Wuest

14. *The Letters of John*, J.R.W. Stott

15. *The Epistles of James and John*, Alexander Ross

16. *Ibid*

17. *The Interpretation of I and II Epistles of Peter, The Three Epistles of John, and The Epistle of Jude*, R.C.H. Lenski

18. *The Letters of John*, J.R.W. Stott

19. *The Epistles of James and John*, Alexander Ross

20. *The Interpretation of I and II Epistles of Peter, The Three Epistles of John, and The Epistle of Jude*, R.C.H. Lenski

21. *The Letters of John*, J.R.W. Stott

22. *In These Last Days*, Kenneth S. Wuest

23. *Ibid*

24. *The Interpretation of I and II Epistles of Peter, The Three Epistles of John, and The Epistle of Jude*, R.C.H. Lenski

25. *The Epistles of James and John*, Alexander Ross

26. *The Letters of John*, J.R.W. Stott

27. *The Interpretation of I and II Epistles of Peter, The Three Epistles of John, and The Epistle of Jude*, R.C.H. Lenski

Chapter Nine, John's Second Letter

1. *In These Last Days*, Kenneth S. Wuest
2. *The Expositors Greek Testament*, David Smith, 1956, Wm.B. Eerdmans, Grand Rapids, Michigan
3. *The Interpretation of I and II Epistles of Peter, The Three Epistles of John, and The Epistle of Jude*, R.C.H. Lenski
4. *In These Last Days*, Kenneth S. Wuest
5. *The Interpretation of I and II Epistles of Peter, The Three Epistles of John, and The Epistle of Jude*, R.C.H. Lenski

Chapter Ten, John's Third Letter

1. *The Letters of John*, J.R.W. Stott
2. *The Epistles of James and John*, Alexander Ross
3. *The Letters of John*, J.W. Roberts, 1968, Sweet Publishing Company, Austin, Texas
4. *The Epistles of James and John*, Alexander Ross
5. *The Letters of John*, J.W. Roberts
6. *The Interpretation of I and II Epistles of Peter, The Three Epistles of John, and The Epistle of Jude*, R.C.H. Lenski

Chapter Eleven, Summary of the Letters

1. *The Expositors Greek Testament*, David Smith
2. *The First Urban Christians*, Wayne A. Meeks

Chapter Twelve, Life in the Later Years

1. *John, Evangelist and Interpreter*, Stephen S. Smalley, 1998, The Intervarsity Press, Downers Grove, Illinois
2. *Ibid*

3. *St. John's Gospel*, R.H. Lightfoot, 1972, Oxford University Press, Oxford

4. *The First Urban Christians*, Wayne A. Meeks

Chapter Thirteen, The Visions

1. *The Twelve Caesars*, Michael Grant

2. *The World of Rome*, Michael Grant

3. *The Divinity of the Roman Emperor*, Lily Ross Taylor, 1931, Scholars Press, Middletown, Connecticut

4. *The Christians as the Romans Saw Them*, Robert Wilken, 2003, Yale University Press, New Haven

5. *The Interpretation of St. John's Revelation*, R.C.H. Lenski, 1961, Augsburg Publishing House, Minneapolis

6. *The Book of Revelation,* Leon Morris, 1999, Wm.B. Eerdmans, Grand Rapids, Michigan

7. *More Than Conquerors*, William Hendriksen, 1970, Baker Book House, Grand Rapids, Michigan

8. *The Revelation to John*, J.W. Roberts, 1974, Sweet Publishing Company, Austin, Texas

9. *Ibid*

10. *The Last Things*, Carl Braaten and Robert Jenson, Editors, 2002, Wm.B.Eerdmans, Grand Rapids, Michigan

11. *The Revelation to John*, J.W. Roberts

12. *Ancient Corinth*, Nicos Papahatzis, 2001, Ekdotike Athenon, Athens

13. *The Greeks*, Kenneth Dover, 1986, The University of Texas Press, Austin

14. *The Greek Way of Death*, Robert Garland, 1985, Cornell University Press, Ithaca, New York

15. *Juvenal, The Sixteen Satires*, Juvenal
16. *Heaven a History*, Collen McDannell and Bernhard Lang, 1988, Yale University Press, New Haven
17. *More Than Conquerors*, William Hendriksen

Chapter Fourteen, After the Visions

1. *Commentary on the Gospel of John*, Frederick L. Godet